Empower Your Journey 365 Affirmations for Self-Esteem and Positive Thoughts

Empower Your Journey 365 Affirmations for Self-Esteem and Positive Thoughts

Daily Inspiration and Reflection for Self-Confidence and Growth for Busy Professionals

Mauricio Vasquez

Be.Bull Publishing

Authors:

Be.Bull Publishing

Mauricio Vasquez

First Printing: December 2024

ISBN 978-1-998402-90-8 (E-book)
ISBN 978-1-998402-89-2 (Hardcover)
ISBN 978-1-998402-88-5 (Paperback)

THANK YOU!

Thank you very much for giving me the opportunity to contribute something positive to your life. I hope this book will help you, and that you will enjoy what you can achieve after reading the positive affirmations. I also hope that this book makes you reflect and that it fills you physically, psychologically, and spiritually. Thank you again!

Please, I want to ask you a small favor.

I do not have a large company, nor do I have a publishing company helping with the marketing and promotion of this book. I wrote and produced this book on my own. As a result, I will be very grateful if you can please give me a review.

With your review, this book can improve its ranking and become more visible to others, so that they can too benefit from it!

To give me your review, please scan this QR code.

Thank you very much in advance for your support!

Mauricio

Empower Your Journey:
Discover More Tools for Success. Scan the QR Code Today

  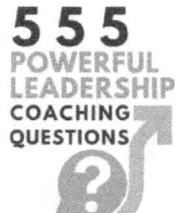 

Table of Contents

Preface 1

Introduction 2

Chapter One: January 4

Chapter Two: February 17

Chapter Three: March 29

Chapter Four: April 42

Chapter Five: May.. 54

Chapter Six: June 67

Chapter Seven: July... 79

Chapter Eight: August.. 92

Chapter Nine: September 105

Chapter Ten: October 117

Chapter Eleven: November 130

Chapter Twelve: December... 142

Conclusion... 155

Preface

It's incredible how quickly an entire year can pass! In the whirlwind of daily responsibilities, reflection on our experiences and the impact they've had on us often gets sidelined. Imagine creating a space each day that inspires your growth, fuels your self-confidence, and deepens your self-awareness—a sanctuary where positive affirmations guide you to discover your potential.

This book has been carefully crafted for you to do just that. Every day, you will encounter an uplifting affirmation designed to energize and inspire your thoughts, while space is provided for you to express your reflections, thoughts, and ideas.

Why a Daily Affirmation Journal?

- **Discover Joy and Inspiration**: Explore what truly lights your path and aligns with your purpose.
- **Harness Positive Thinking**: Channel your thoughts to work for you, cultivating a mindset that welcomes growth and opportunities.
- **Prioritize Self-Care**: Empower yourself by making time to care for your mental, emotional, and physical well-being.

Each affirmation invites you to pause, focus, and engage in a dialogue with yourself. This journey is not about perfection but about progress—nurturing a steady, one-day-at-a-time rhythm that honors your growth and helps you make meaningful choices.

This is more than a journal; it's a companion for your self-care and self-discovery journey. As you write, you'll uncover layers of insight, wisdom, and strength. The act of journaling itself becomes transformative, allowing you to visualize and create a future rooted in clarity and confidence.

How to Use This Journal

1. Start each day by reading the positive affirmation provided.
2. Take a moment to reflect on its meaning in your life today.
3. Use the space provided to write down your thoughts, insights, or ideas that arise.
4. Let this practice serve as a mindful ritual, grounding you and propelling you forward.

Let this book be your trusted guide through the year—a source of daily encouragement, a space for reflection, and a tool for building a brighter, stronger you. Together, let's embrace the extraordinary within the ordinary and make this year truly transformative.

You are worth this daily investment. Let's begin this journey of growth, one affirmation at a time.

Introduction

When was the last time you allowed yourself a moment of pure positivity? Not just a fleeting thought, but a true pause—a moment of connection with your inner self. Positive affirmations are like beacons; they guide us, nurture our confidence, and inspire us to embrace change. They remind us of our strength, validate our worth, and illuminate the path toward growth.

The science behind this is compelling. Our minds are powerful, but they often need a gentle nudge to overcome negativity, doubt, and external influences. Positive affirmations provide that nudge, helping us to realign our thoughts, believe in our abilities, and visualize a future filled with possibilities.

Every day presents an opportunity to reflect, grow, and reconnect with who we truly are. This book offers a framework for that journey—365 daily affirmations designed to uplift, inspire, and invite self-reflection. These affirmations aren't just words; they are catalysts for discovering the power within you.

Why This Book?

Negativity acts like clutter, holding us back and clouding our vision. Daily affirmations work as a clearing mechanism, creating space for clarity, confidence, and courage. This journal allows you to take those affirmations a step further by offering dedicated space to explore your thoughts, insights, and revelations inspired by each affirmation.

This book is for anyone seeking a space to:

- Rediscover their inner strength.
- Reflect on their daily experiences and emotions.
- Cultivate a consistent, mindful practice of self-discovery.

Whether you use this journal as a way to start your day with intention or wind down with reflection, its purpose is to be your companion in building a life of positivity and purpose.

How to Use This Book

Every day, you will find:

1. **A Positive Affirmation**: Read it with intention. Let its message settle in your mind and heart. Reflect on what it means for you today.
2. **Space for Reflection**: Write down your thoughts, insights, or ideas. Whether it's a sentence, a paragraph, or a stream of consciousness, let your reflections flow freely.

This journey is uniquely yours. Feel free to approach the book in whatever way resonates with you. Begin on the current date and continue from there, or explore affirmations at random. The only rule is to engage authentically and wholeheartedly.

The Transformative Power of Reflection

Reflection amplifies the power of affirmations. It helps you uncover patterns, identify aspirations, and clarify values. Writing down your reflections allows you to see your growth over time. This process isn't about perfection; it's about showing up for yourself, one day at a time.

Each affirmation is crafted to touch on universal themes of self-worth, resilience, gratitude, and purpose. You may find that some affirmations resonate deeply, while others offer new perspectives. Both are valuable. The goal is to spark a dialogue with yourself—a dialogue that encourages growth, heals wounds, and strengthens your belief in your potential.

Remember, This Is Your Journey

Obstacles may arise, but remember that each one presents a choice: to stay stagnant or to grow. This journal is a reminder that you have the power to choose growth. One affirmation, one reflection, one day at a time—you are creating a brighter, stronger version of yourself.

Take this opportunity to invest in your well-being. Allow these affirmations to inspire you, guide you, and unlock your potential. The year ahead is a blank canvas, and you hold the brush.

Let's begin. This is your way.

Chapter One: January

January is commonly the month where I can start afresh and look to the upcoming year, but the original meaning sheds some light on something often overlooked. The Roman god, *Janus*, is where this month's name is derived from. He had two faces; one that looked forward and another looking back. These features signified that while I should look to the future and prepare myself, it is just as important to look back and reflect on the road so far.

While it is fine to make resolutions at the beginning of every year, maybe this time around, I focus on *myself* and use these upcoming months to inspire and better myself bit by bit. The journey is well worth the end, plus the growth along the way is inspiring.

All that starts right here, and it can't begin without the first day...

JANUARY 1

I will trust myself to have the strength I need to take on risks and the upcoming challenges. Trust is about me having an optimistic and realistic belief in my true, inherent potential; both actualized and not yet actualized.

JANUARY 2

My journey is centered on learning as much as I can about my personal growth and development. Learning is where my progress begins; learning about myself and the world around me.

JANUARY 3

Every challenge I experience in life is a chance to be taught and an opportunity to grow and live with more purpose. My purpose is something bigger than myself—going beyond my needs—it is what will pull me into action. It is my compelling reason to be and do in this world.

JANUARY 4

My strengths and gifts are my own; they will help me create a meaningful life. My strengths are the assets that I can tap into in times of difficulty. They are a source of my resilience.

JANUARY 5

The way in which I choose to start my morning can arm me to conquer the day ahead. How I start my day affects how the rest of my day will go, taking me closer or further away from what I want to accomplish in the day.

JANUARY 6

I will not allow other people's opinions of me to shape how I live my own life. My independence increases my self-value and self-esteem.

JANUARY 7

The goals I set today will end up forming who my future self is. Goals are how I translate my dreams into reality.

JANUARY 8

Keeping a healthy mindset will help shape my understanding of both my possibilities and my limitations. A healthy mindset means that I am looking for solutions instead of focusing on my problems. A healthy mindset includes learning from my mistakes.

JANUARY 9

The more intentional I live my life according to my values, the more open I will be to having fulfillment and satisfaction. My personal values are a central part of who I am and who I want to be.

JANUARY 10

Knowing myself means understanding my strengths individually and how they can work in connection with each other to continue my self-improvement. My strengths include my knowledge, attributes, skills, and talents that I can do well.

JANUARY 11

The more genuine I am with myself, the more authentic I can be in my expressions and how I relate to others.

JANUARY 12

I will see the world as hopeful, even amid challenges. I will see the world as where I have a place of purpose and possibilities.

JANUARY 13

Even though it might not always be easy, I will let myself learn through trial and error. The most important life lessons I will ever learn will be from the poor decisions I make.

JANUARY 14

An essential part of setting my goals is understanding my reality and what does and doesn't work best for me. I will set goals for myself, not goals for what others expect. My goals must be grounded in my purpose and vision.

JANUARY 15

My life is not summed up by one moment or one experience. I am more than just what has happened to me, and I have control over my future.

JANUARY 16

All the change that I am purposefully manifesting starts with my awareness. My awareness is about the present state, and where I am right now.

JANUARY 17

I will find the courage to step outside of my comfort zone by understanding that it relies on my belief in myself. Stepping out of my comfort zone helps me live life at its fullest and mature and grow as an individual.

JANUARY 18

As I make decisions in life, it creates a map that displays and reflects my values. This will help me learn more about myself, what matters to me, and what truly drives me.

JANUARY 19

I will not allow the "What Ifs" and "Yeah Buts" to constrain the powerful changes I decide to put into practice. Limiting beliefs are thoughts and opinions that I believe to be the truth, but have a negative impact by stopping me from moving forward.

JANUARY 20

Having a realistic view of my capabilities is what will start creating an optimistic trust in myself and what I can do. My capabilities are skills and abilities that I do well and that I bring to the table as a person, student, or professional.

JANUARY 21

It is far better for me to listen more and ask better questions. Questions breathe life into knowledge, and both of these enrich my life. When I do all these things, I shall be better and more diverse for it.

JANUARY 22

It is vital to have relationships built on collaboration. My life is made on the contributions of many, not just my own. When I fully accept this, I will discover new aspects of myself I didn't realize before.

JANUARY 23

My life's experience comprises both enjoyment and fulfillment. The things I do and learn about, what I love to do, are where my enjoyment is. The quality of the person I am becoming and what I bring to the world; that is my fulfillment.

JANUARY 24

Whatever I achieve or do not accomplish in this life is my responsibility. I will hold myself accountable and celebrate when I win, and learn when I lose. There is no room for denial

JANUARY 25

I will not let the things that happen around me control what happens in my own life. My environment does not get to define, control, or create who I am. I take ownership of everything in my domain, including the outcome and everything that affects it.

JANUARY 26

I have the power within me. I will learn how to access that power to become more intentional, be more committed, and inspire myself to action!

JANUARY 27

When I challenge myself, I will not do it simply for the sake of it. I will be purposeful and use my capabilities to fuel my response to the challenges.

JANUARY 28

A purposeful life is a choice I can and will make each day. I will make it my energy source, directional compass, and how I shape my life. A purposeful life is when I am moving towards a big goal in my life that aligns with my values, passions and makes me happy.

JANUARY 29

The best way to achieve the dreams and goals I have is to remain committed to my beliefs and the actions I choose to take. I will reach what I set out to accomplish by holding myself to what I commit myself to do every day.

January 30

The world is filled with more than enough limitations. I will not place them on myself; instead, I choose to see my full potential realized for myself and for my loved ones. My limitations are not objective breaking points; they are just what I choose to believe to be the limit.

Life is made up of choices, from when I wake up to when I fall asleep. I will strive to make the best decisions for my growth and use those choices to become the version of myself I am aiming for. Every decision count to move me forward or backwards.

Every month there will be a time meant for looking back over the inspirations I found, progress, or areas that need change. In this space, I can jot down notes on my thoughts, summarize the month, or specify the impacts that came from my daily moments with myself.

As always, it is my absolute best that I am aiming for, and times to reflect can be where we find the most inspiration.

<u>Monthly Reflections</u>

What did this last month mean to me?

What daily inspiration had the most meaning to me?

This month I learned...

Chapter Two: February

February gets a bad rap for being sort of a "let-down month" because of all the attention that January gets with resolutions and the New Year. Some people even misspell it and get frustrated, not to mention that it's the shortest month. All that can make it challenging to continue any momentum from January. There must be a better way to enjoy a month as fantastic as February can be.

Let's do away with the old attitude and go into this next month with a positive mindset and a belief that February can be even better than the one before. There is the chance to reflect and have the opportunity to both remember and see where I want to be as I improve. It's a month of Valentine's, Julius Caesar, and the elusive Leap Year day.

Carry the mindset of possibility and new perspectives going forward so that each month is a chance to become better than I was.

FEBRUARY 1

I will keep my mindset of living purposefully by remembering that life will happen for me, not simply to me. The first one takes me in a direction of deeper growth, learning and healing. The second one leads me down a path of victimhood and martyrdom.

FEBRUARY 2

Choice is the cornerstone of what makes me alive. In my humanity is the freedom and responsibility that comes with that kind of choice. I will endeavor each day to fully appreciate that. Choice is not just about choosing among the existing options; it is also about creating new ones.

FEBRUARY 3

Life isn't just about me; there is a world filled with valid and different perspectives. Being able to appreciate that and grow by exploring other views is an important part of my process. I can remain true to my core beliefs and still learn from how others see life.

FEBRUARY 4

My learning is not anyone else's responsibility. In order for me to grow, I must take advantage of the opportunities to learn, while maintaining my integrity and being authentic. Learning will allow me to adapt, to survive and thrive in this new era.

FEBRUARY 5

Accountability is one of the most important characteristics of change. Being accountable bridges the gap between my intentions and the actions I end up taking. Without it, I will not grow to my full potential.

FEBRUARY 6

I will not allow my situation to define the choices I end up making. Instead, I will take initiative and action to create my own path with decisions based on what is best for me and my future.

FEBRUARY 7

The closer I get to understanding my purpose and my mission on this earth, the more complete my life shall be. My purpose is my path that provides orientation. I will strive to learn and evolve so that each experience I have can be as fulfilling as possible.

FEBRUARY 8

Where I place my attention in life is where the most growth and progress occur. In my work, at home, and with my relationships, I will strive for balance so that my growth is spread out and my life flourishes.

FEBRUARY 9

Curiosity does not have to be a negative aspect of my character. I can use my curiosity to drive my attention, my desire to explore, the risks I am willing to take, and the knowledge I open myself up to. I will learn how to use my experiences to continue feeding my curiosity, and from that feeding my process and growth.

FEBRUARY 10

My awareness of both myself and the world around me is key in shaping both who I am and who I will become. Using my awareness, I can expand my experiences, take more effective actions in my life, and trust that my path is leading me in the right direction.

FEBRUARY 11

The experiences of those around me are not only valid, but they are excellent resources to learn about the perspectives of others. I will continue to learn from their advice, expertise, and backgrounds rather than viewing it as an obstacle in my own experience. Learning from other people's mistakes and successes is an efficient way for me to figure things out on my own.

FEBRUARY 12

I set my pace, the world does not set it for me. I will make time for reflection so that what I learn can be fully embraced and absorbed. I will not be made to feel guilty about prioritizing my growth and health over an expected pace of life.

FEBRUARY 13

My life isn't just about choosing what is already there, it is about setting new goals, blazing trails, and new experiences. What makes my life spectacular isn't what I am doing, but who I am while I am doing it. The person I am becoming will create options for myself, and not simply accept what exists.

FEBRUARY 14

Love is not an obstacle, nor does it hold me back. I am the person I am because of the love I have received, and because of that, I can now do the same for others. Life is not just about knowledge and experience, it is about love as well; for others, for myself, and for the journey.

FEBRUARY 15

My attitude can help or hurt my situation. I cannot expect to flourish if my attitude doesn't match. From now on I will pay more attention to my mindset and how it is setting me up for either success or struggle. By taking responsibility for these outcomes, I will gain more control in my life.

FEBRUARY 16

Part of understanding who I am as a person is being truthful about the strengths and gifts I have. By uplifting myself and viewing my characteristics through a positive lens, I will learn how to appreciate all parts of the person I am, and who I am becoming.

FEBRUARY 17

My strengths in life don't grow and become stronger on their own. It is my responsibility to not only recognize my strengths, but to hone them, value them, and learn all I can about them. The more knowledge I have about my strengths, the better I can use them throughout this journey.

FEBRUARY 18

My purpose is not what I do, but who I am being. Understanding my purpose and meaning in life is not a singular moment, it is an ongoing conversation. Every day I add more to the dialogue, but it is never fully finished. I need to be dynamic and purposeful in my actions

FEBRUARY 19

Self-care deserves to be a priority in my life. My wellbeing will rely on being balanced in my mental, physical, and emotional state. Unless I recognize the importance of addressing each aspect, I am not truly balanced.

FEBRUARY 20

The actions I put forth in my life deserve excellence. I will let myself be guided by my desire to be committed to bringing excellence to everything I do. Every day is a chance to put my best into the world. Doing your best means never stop trying.

FEBRUARY 21

I will learn to trust my intuition and do so through the rule of three: be open to what I feel, speak it into existence, and trust it to come into being. I am capable of building this trust with myself.

FEBRUARY 22

The positivity I can bring to the world is not contained to one part of my life. I will commit to creating change on a positive level through the conversations and relationships I have.

FEBRUARY 23

I recognize that my life affects more than just me. The influence I have must be both wholesome and positive. It starts with me and ripples outward, but it is my responsibility to be aware of how I utilize my influence.

FEBRUARY 24

My assumptions are there to be questioned for me to have a greater grasp on reality. I will not let those assumptions become my mindset, instead, I will be objective and methodical in testing my assumptions to find out their truthfulness.

FEBRUARY 25

I am creating change every single day. I am doing this through my ambition, my drive to be better, the ability to self-start, and how I am capable of taking charge. These characteristics are my tools that will build what I am working towards.

FEBRUARY 26

My positivity and optimism will enable me to make the most out of whatever situation I find myself in. By being consistent in both those characteristics, I am setting myself up to succeed and make positive impacts. My optimism can protect me against sadness and anxiety.

FEBRUARY 27

When I give myself the time and freedom to reflect on the things I have learned, I open myself to new depths of learning. When I do reflect, I will do so without judgment and start the work on what I discover about myself without negativity.

FEBRUARY 28

When I discover new things about myself that need to be worked on I will use the situation to my advantage. Each of those moments is an opportunity to consider my choices, where I currently am, and what I can do differently.

FEBRUARY 29 (Leap Year)

When I acknowledge the pace I need to be at, despite what the world says, I will use this for my benefit. Slowing down or taking a break is important in recovering from my work and responsibilities. This will fuel my progress and become the reasons my dreams come true.

Monthly Reflections

What did this last month mean to me?

What daily inspiration had the most meaning to me?

This month I learned...

Chapter Three: March

This entire journey through daily inspiration is all about refreshing and renewing myself. In the spirit of that, did I know that March was the beginning of a new year for quite some time—even as late as the 1750s? Instead of just letting that be another historical fact, I'll use it as another chance to have a beginning. January, and sometimes December, tends to be where I could go for reflection, but that is a change that can be made here and now.

How many times have I reached the month of March and felt some significance? It's important to not let any of these moments become usual or commonplace. The world might not give March its due, but for a month named after the Roman god of war, I would think a little more respect would be in order.

So, in this period where Spring begins and I have a brand-new beginning all over again, build from there. Each day, take in the inspiration and remember that a fresh start can come at any time.

MARCH 1

Being self-aware means knowing about both the good and the bad. I will use my awareness to enhance my strengths and work on my weaknesses. I am not weaker by acknowledging where I need to focus more attention.

MARCH 2

My purpose is not just about me. True satisfaction is found when my purpose encompasses both myself and one that is beyond me alone. Purpose is related to how I will show up and BE with those people around me.

MARCH 3

I am learning to let go of my need to look good when it is to my detriment. I will also work towards not needing to always be right. My need for both these things gets in the way of the journey I am on.

MARCH 4

The gifts and strengths that are within me are unique to my experience. If I focus on developing my strengths, I can grow faster than when trying to improve my weaknesses. I will go into each day committed to using them to create a meaningful life.

MARCH 5

My purpose is bigger than what I can imagine. It is not contained to a strategy or goal; it is a living, changing entity. Seeking my purpose will draw meaningful goals and strategies to me, but neither defines what my purpose is. I will treat it like what it is; fundamental to my existence.

MARCH 6

I will be more aware of how I treat and respond to my emotions. They are not my enemy, nor are they a detriment to my journey. I will learn how to understand my emotions and use them as positive information along the way. My emotions help me to know what I need and want (or don't want).

MARCH 7

I will focus on what is happening to me now. My present is where I can bring about change. I will learn from my past, and work towards my future—but I will live in the present.

MARCH 8

There is no such thing as a moment in which there is nothing I can do. Even though I might not be able to take action or change the situation, I can help myself and others during it. Just because I can't do what I would like to, doesn't mean I can't make the situation better.

MARCH 9

I can't control everything. There will be times when things happen, and I will have no control over them and I accept this. Even though I may not be able to control it, I can control my reaction to the situation. That is power in itself, and I will work on recognizing that.

MARCH 10

I will not assume that I am doing everything right. By taking the time to check, I will make sure that my attention is where it should be. It is my responsibility to ensure that my focus is on essential parts of my life that are within my control. I will not waste any more energy on things I cannot change or control.

MARCH 11

I take my responsibilities seriously. In everything I do, I strive to bring my absolute best. My resourcefulness and authenticity are tools I can use to my advantage. When I allow my best parts to work together, I can create real change.

MARCH 12

Self-care matters in my life. When I am not at my best, I run the risk of not bringing everything I have. My state of being and well-being affect my mindset and abilities. I will do better at recognizing when self-care needs to be made more of a priority in my life.

MARCH 13

My goals, whether they are big or small, rely on my motivation to make them a reality. I will use my small goals as building blocks to manifest my bigger goals. I will keep small goals simple and achievable so that I can feel the momentum of small wins.

MARCH 14

My goals are there to help me advance my life and purpose. They are not there to give me a reason to break myself down. If I do not complete a goal, I am not a failure. I do not measure myself based on the number of goals I set and reach. I measure my success based on the person I was and who I am now. If I improve, then I succeed.

MARCH 15

In order to grow as a person, I must learn to set aside what I think I know and replace it with what I actually do know. Holding on to old ways of thinking will only keep me from the new knowledge I am aiming for.

MARCH 16

I can start working towards increasing the wisdom in my life at any time I desire. The foundation for this is created when I have more questions and fewer answers. Sometimes my questions are more important than the answers.

MARCH 17

Where I am right now is not a place of completion. I am a work in progress, and that is something I do not judge myself for. I will continue to adapt and evolve as my life progresses, but I am never a finished product.

MARCH 18

While it is important to listen to productive self-criticism, I will not let my inner critic control me. I will be aware of the difference between advice and judgment, especially when it comes to me. I won't allow myself to be the judge, jury, and executioner.

MARCH 19

When I am clear in my commitments and responsibilities, it goes a long way toward helping me be guided by my purpose. I understand that intentional living will shape the direction of my life. My intentional living is about creating healthy boundaries.

MARCH 20

My strengths can be fuel for my responsibilities. When I learn to combine the two and let them work for each other, I will be contributing to my overall well-being. I will focus on doing the right things and doing things right.

MARCH 21

I will not have goals just for the sake of having them. Creating meaningful goals that are fulfilled through intentional living will lead to satisfaction in knowing I make progress. With having meaningful goals, I am more likely to stay motivated and accomplish my objectives.

MARCH 22

Many things are positives in my life and help me grow; fear and anxiety are not in that category. Neither contribute to productive learning and will only weigh me down. I will not be constricted by negative characteristics, instead choosing a better focus for my attention.

MARCH 23

My awareness is one of the key tools to finding and understanding my purpose. By recognizing that, utilizing reflection and self-inquiry, I will be more prepared for a journey of excellence, and deeper meaning in my work and life.

MARCH 24

I have the freedom to choose, but I also must recognize the responsibility that comes with that. My choice may be mine, but that does not mean that there won't be results from that choice—positive or negative. The more I understand this, the wiser my choices will become.

MARCH 25

In a chaotic world, my principles are what can ground me in reality and my journey. By understanding those truths, I can lead a more wholesome and effective life. My principles are my moral rules or beliefs that help me know what is right and wrong, and that influence my actions.

MARCH 26

I recognize the power of attention to detail. By taking greater care to notice the usually missed details in my life, I can find a greater and deeper understanding of my reality. My reality is the sum of noticed and unnoticed details.

MARCH 27

I understand that every situation might not be able to be fixed, but I also recognize that each situation is workable. When I take the time to consider the possible solutions, I will be able to work on the problem instead of assuming it can't be fixed.

MARCH 28

Every day, I will strive to create a world where there is freedom and safety for each person. I will not only do this through my actions but also through my mentality and attitude—even amid difficulty.

MARCH 29

I understand that in life, there will be challenges. I am willing to take risks and make difficult choices in order to overcome those challenges. Even when it isn't easy, I will strive to be victorious in those times of hardship.

MARCH 30

Life isn't just about one view. When I can see things from multiple perspectives, I will be able to bring wisdom to the issues and problems I encounter. My wisdom is best viewed from the multiple perspectives I can access.

Good things in life do not just happen. In order for me to obtain consistent positive and productive results in my life, I must do three things well; prepare, execute, and follow through. When I commit to all these steps, I will be setting myself up for continued success.

Monthly Reflections

What did this last month mean to me?

_____

_____

_____

_____

What daily inspiration had the most meaning to me?

_____

_____

_____

_____

This month I learned...

_____

_____

_____

_____

Chapter Four: April

This month is like opening a box filled with all different kinds of snacks and trinkets because there is so much happening! You have a day dedicated to pranks, one dedicated to trees, there is of course, Easter, and a day celebrating Earth itself. Quite ambitious to pack so much into one month, but April gets it done and does it in style!

With so much going on, it might seem difficult to find a theme, but with every special day and event, there is one overarching ideal that shines through; *love*. You can start with the month being named after Aphrodite, who is known for being love manifested. Spring brings with it the sense of refreshment and renewal, but also new love that is "in the air" throughout the month. Throw in that the birthstone is a diamond, and you can see how April is the month that puts love right out in front.

Let's use every day as a new chance to learn more about love, and how it can be shown to ourselves and others!

APRIL 1

I understand the potential for my actions to either progress or hinder my journey. When I live with an attitude of awareness, my actions will not only set me up for success, they will display my true intentions.

APRIL 2

Being flexible, especially in moments of difficulty, will enable me to thrive regardless of what is going on around me. I can function in a wide variety of contexts and situations. The more I can adapt, the more I will rise above.

APRIL 3

I allow my values and principles to dictate my actions, rather than allow outside influences to do so. When my beliefs and ethics are in line with reality and truth, I can trust them to send me in the right direction. Finding consistency in choosing my principles is one of the most important lessons I can learn.

APRIL 4

Living a full life means understanding that the learning never stops. I will put in the effort to ensure that my desire to learn never diminishes, but also to find ways that will improve how I learn. Being devoted to my self-education shows faith in myself.

APRIL 5

Opportunities in life will not be handed to me, so I will open my eyes to see each chance that life brings to me. I understand that when I open my eyes and identify those opportunities, my growth will exponentially increase as well. The first step I can take towards having a brighter life must be to increase the awareness I have of my surroundings.

APRIL 6

The tasks I set for myself and the ones that work towards my self-improvement are necessary, important, and deserve my attention. I will strive to build my discipline so that I can stay on task and continue my personal growth.

APRIL 7

Every experience in my life is a new chance to learn and grow. I will revel and take joy in the positive, but also gain understanding and perspective from the negative results. When everything is a learning opportunity, I can overcome anything. In a life of valleys and mountains, there is value in seeing value all around.

APRIL 8

My life is about balance. I will find safety and refreshment in my comfort zone, but I will not live my life in that place. I will push myself, take risks, and learn to grow. When I can exist in both the comfort zone and the places that challenge me then I will find true personal growth.

APRIL 9

To progress in life, I do not have to know everything about everything. I recognize the value in not having all the answers, and being able to grow in life despite that. I will not allow my curiosity to become a hindrance. Being able to accept the unknown is a valuable lesson for me to learn.

APRIL 10

I will challenge the assumptions in my life and use different perspectives to nurture new ideas. When I do not rely on what I think I know, and instead discover what is real, I can find previously unseen possibilities. Living outside of my own opinion is a healthy practice to adopt. This means finding value in what other people think and seeking to understand why they have those opinions.

APRIL 11

Acknowledging reality will go a long way toward creating a true perspective of my life. I will recognize what I have done, come to terms with what I have not done, and work to learn and be aware of what the future can be. I do not benefit from staying in a vacuum of my thoughts.

APRIL 12

I understand that learning is not always an easy process. I must be willing to be challenged and stretched past where I am comfortable to learn certain aspects of life. By accepting and recognizing this truth, I am more prepared for when those lessons arrive.

APRIL 13

I recognize that because of the need for balance I must find value in both optimism and seeing reality. I do not need to choose one or the other. By crafting my perspective around both of these views I can have a well-rounded, strong approach to life.

APRIL 14

I will not get bogged down by frustration amid a situation. Instead, I will become agile and able to adapt as the circumstances shift around me. When I can adjust to the demands, even as they change, I will be able to avoid unnecessary stress and grow from each experience.

APRIL 15

I am not powerless over my habits. The ability to change and improve is completely within my control. My awareness and strength will help me know which choices are right for me.

APRIL 16

The relationships in my life are a gift. Even when challenging times come, I will not forget that the people I love and those who love me are what matter.

APRIL 17

What I can accomplish and the belief I have in myself are interconnected. Whatever challenges or difficulties come my way, if I truly believe in my ability to conquer it, then I shall. There is power in believing in myself.

APRIL 18

Finding success in my work is all about balance. Being able to invest myself in my profession means understanding the importance of investing in my personal life as well. Taking care of myself will only work for my benefit in all aspects of my life—profession included.

APRIL 19

I am worth my own attention and focus. By including self-care in my routine, I prove to myself that it matters. Every time I prioritize my well being I bring increased balance to my life, which improves it overall.

APRIL 20

The little things in life are sometimes the most memorable. Just because something isn't considered "productive" doesn't mean it doesn't add richness to my life. Enjoyments like hobbies are not only beneficial, they give me a glimpse into different perspectives.

APRIL 21

Because my time is valuable, the way in which I use it really does matter. Whether it is too much work or too much play, having control over where my time goes means having control over the balance of my own life. Having opportunities to manage my time is a blessing and will benefit me in the long and short term.

APRIL 22

I will learn the different ways to love those around me, and myself. The way I express love towards those in my life has meaning, so I will put effort into loving people as individuals and not simply in general.

APRIL 23

Being happy is just as important a part of my life as any other pursuit. Feeling joy is something that I not only deserve but also strive to incorporate into my daily situations. When I only look for the negative, that is what manifests, so I shall seek the positive and my happiness.

APRIL 24

Life is filled with chances to be brave in the face of difficulties. I have courage and bravery inside me, even if I feel fear in situations. Just because I am afraid or trepidatious about something doesn't mean I can't be brave—there isn't courage without fear.

APRIL 25

Just because something didn't happen when I wanted it to, doesn't mean it isn't going to happen. My timing isn't the standard, and the more I recognize that the more energy I can save. Being attentive, focused, and motivated means more than needing something to happen right away—if it means I have to wait.

APRIL 26

Balance isn't just about work and personal life, it also means putting weight in my dreams and goals. Even if something feels far off and out of reach, by believing that my dream is worthwhile and attainable I will achieve it one day. All that can only happen when I allow myself the freedom to dream in the first place.

APRIL 27

In the pace and hustle of life, I cannot forget that taking care of my physical self is just as important as my emotional self-care. The more I treat my body with respect and positive attention, the more I show myself that I am a person of value. The way I treat myself—inside and outside—matters in the way I view myself.

APRIL 28

My words matter, but my actions will reflect who I truly am. I recognize that the habits I choose to keep and those to change will contribute to the person I end up becoming—and who I am right now.

APRIL 29

I am not in this life alone; the people I choose to love and surround myself with have an influence on me. By seeing value in myself I will set out to also remove the negative influences that have been impacting me.

APRIL 30

When I let doubt cloud my expectations of myself and life I am not setting myself up for success. The more belief I let in, the more doubt will be removed, making room for progress, productivity, and success. Beginning from a place of belief makes all the difference.

Monthly Reflections

What did this last month mean to me?

_____

_____

_____

_____

_____

What daily inspiration had the most meaning to me?

_____

_____

_____

_____

_____

This month I learned...

_____

_____

_____

_____

_____

Chapter Five: May

Since the days of the early Roman Calendar, the month of May has been known for renewal and fresh beginnings. The snow has thawed, animals are waking up from hibernation, and the first day of Spring cannot wait to shine once again. Do you know what the best thing about May is? That it can mean so many wonderful things for each of us—that means you as well.

What places in your life need reexamining? Are there emotional spring cleanings that should be taking place? How about dreams and goals that you have yet to tackle? When it comes to refreshing ourselves and the theme of *renewal* it doesn't have to be confined to one thing or one area of your life. So, in the spirit of beginnings and taking on new things, move forward ready to learn about yourself and where your life is going.

MAY 1

Living a positive, fulfilling life means understanding that the learning process never ends. The more open I am to accepting life lessons—new or adjusting my thinking on the old—the better my life will become overall. I will strive to avoid stagnating, instead of pushing to always learn more.

MAY 2

I will recognize the place that creativity has in life. It isn't just about art or creating things, it is about finding those little, special places in life that matter to me. By recognizing the importance of being creative and growing that part of myself, I will be honing balanced well-being both now and in the future.

MAY 3

The way I view time matters. If I am constantly negative and stressed about how much time there is—or how little time—then I am not creating an environment for positive growth. However, if I approach time with patience and a positive attitude I can create a more healthy relationship with how I manage time.

MAY 4

Self-control is very important in life, but I also need to be aware of where it should be applied. There is a difference between self-control and not wanting to take a risk for the sake of protecting myself. By strengthening my awareness I am also making sure that I know what is too much of a good thing, and when I should try something new and bold.

MAY 5

Love is not meant to be confined to just one area of my life. I can cultivate love in my home, within my profession, in my friendships, and in the activities I enjoy experiencing. I will work towards being more open and letting love into all the aspects of my life. Love makes me stronger.

MAY 6

Just as it is important to find purpose in my work, it is just as vital for me to find those places where I can seek my happiness on a different level. Whether it is a hobby or some other enjoyment, there is nothing selfish about wanting to experience these places of happiness by myself. I will remember to make room for those happy areas in my life.

MAY 7

Succeeding in life isn't just about having a positive attitude, it is also about being brave enough to push through everything in the way. I will not let fear stop me from achieving what I have set out to do, and my courage will help me navigate those challenges.

MAY 8

I believe that the goals I have are worth working towards. I know that there will be times when I will want to rush, but in those moments, I will remember that patience calms the chaos. When I can bring a patient attitude to my daily life, I will be setting myself up for continued success.

MAY 9

There is room for both reality and my dreams to exist together. I can aim for the sky and dream big, but also be grounded and pragmatic. With belief in myself and awareness of my strengths and weaknesses, I can be real while not lessening my dreams.

MAY 10

My mental health is not something for me to hide or apologize for. I will remember that I do not have to adjust who I am for anyone else, and that includes my mental health. When I can prioritize myself instead of what others think, I am truly on the path to living a healthy life.

MAY 11

When I choose to overlook negative habits instead of confronting them, I am seeing my future self as a priority. While it might be easier to let those things slide, when I take responsibility and bring improvement to those areas I am saying that my personal growth is worth it.

MAY 12

The best way for me to grow as a person is to surround myself with people who can teach me. Even though it may be easier to interact with people who do not challenge me, I must not miss out on the chance for growth simply because it takes less effort. The relationships in my life have an impact on me, and because I can control who is in my life I can decide whether that impact is positive or not, and whether I am being open to learning new lessons or not.

MAY 13

Belief, regarding the people I surround myself with, can be a circular thing. It is important for me to believe in myself, but for those I love it is just as important for me to believe in them. Understanding this will help me remember that I am not alone, and that where I place my belief matters. For when I believe in others, those I love will also believe in me.

MAY 14

There is nothing wrong with being deeply invested in a multitude of hobbies, just as there isn't anything wrong with being fully dedicated to my profession. The important key to that balance is recognizing when action is needed to correct that balance. When I can honestly confront those corrections and follow through rather than ignore them, I will have a better grasp of what true balance in life is.

MAY 15

There isn't room in my life for both proper self-care and guilt over taking the time for it. When I make the time to rest and give attention to my physical and emotional self, it is so I can press on afterward. Guilt will just negate the rest I am striving for, so by removing it and accepting self-care as a priority in my life I am choosing a healthy future for me and my loved ones.

MAY 16

I will start to see creativity as a valuable asset of my life. When I make room for my creativity, I am putting worth in how I express myself. This will expand my emotional IQ and pave the way for further creative growth. My creativity is a source for increasing confidence in my potential.

MAY 17

My priorities are a window into what I value in life. Understanding this will allow me to invest my attention and resources into what really matters to me. When I am more aware of this process, I can see if there are areas of my life in which I need to readdress some priorities.

MAY 18

It is important for me to understand that my perspective does not negate how others feel; I may think they understand how I feel about them, but that is not the reality. Understanding that, I will begin paying more attention to whether I tell others what they mean to me or if I continue assuming they know. By recognizing the difference between knowing I love someone and actually telling them I love them, I am willing to see from their point of view and not just my own.

MAY 19

Finding things in life that I enjoy and seeking happiness are lifelong endeavors. By keeping myself aware and open to new interests and joys, I will begin discovering happiness and learning lessons in places that I hadn't seen before.

MAY 20

Courage is an aspect of my character with a diverse number of applications in my life. The more I recognize that, the more areas of my life I am willing to be courageous in. Courage is needed to love, to change, to try new things, to make hard choices; understanding this will strengthen all parts of myself.

MAY 21

There are people in my life who see me in a leadership role, so the example I set matters. By understanding how I am seen and the influence I have I can learn more about myself and the kind of leader I am and want to be.

MAY 22

The more I want to rush the process of things in my life, the less I will be able to learn from the journey. Patience isn't just about being willing to wait, it means putting in the work so that when I reach my goal, I am prepared to fully embrace, understand, and enjoy it.

MAY 23

The important part about having dreams is that I do not lose hope when things don't go the way I expected. However, it is normal if that happens. While it is vital to have goals, dreams allow me to believe that I am capable of more than just the logical and possible.

MAY 24

Integrity means that I hold myself to the same ethics when I am in private as I do when I am in public. Consistency across all those aspects of my life creates a healthy balance. Achieving consistency is about loving not only the targeted results, but also the process.

MAY 25

It is more important for me to be honest with myself about what I need to adjust in my life rather than avoiding difficult changes. The more transparency I have with myself, the more I set myself up for positive and productive changes.

MAY 26

Even though sometimes the work ahead of me seems insurmountable, I am capable of succeeding. By taking these situations one step, one moment, and one action at a time, I am building habits that will help me in the future. Step by step I will be able to improve my confidence and results.

MAY 27

The depth of the relationships that I have are parallel to the investment I have in them. The people I choose to give my time and attention to will be the relationships that are the closest and most important to me. By seeing my time as valuable, I will be more discerning with my close relationships. Not all relationships are meant to last.

MAY 28

Belief is an important part of life. Whether it is my belief in myself, something bigger than me, the people in my life, or simply belief in positivity, it matters. By allowing myself the freedom to believe, I put my strengths into my purpose.

MAY 29

The skills, ability, expertise, and work ethic I bring to my profession are valuable; and their combination makes me unique. There is nothing wrong with wanting a healthy work environment where those traits of mine are recognized and appreciated. I deserve to feel needed.

May 30

Being aware of my self-care means doing what is necessary for my overall health, not only what I want to do. I will be committed to being attentive to all the ways I need to care for my well-being. The more I invest in this balance, the more natural it will become.

I can combat the areas of frustration in my life with a willingness to learn. When I stop giving my focus to the problem and begin investing it in learning how to handle the situation, I will find solutions. The lower the frustration in my life, the more open my vision is to opportunities to grow.

Monthly Reflections

What did this last month mean to me?

_____

_____

_____

_____

What daily inspiration had the most meaning to me?

_____

_____

_____

_____

This month I learned...

_____

_____

_____

_____

Chapter Six: June

June is unique in that it was once half of a large, more seasonal period of time known as Liao. The change in weather that signaled the end of Spring brought with it hotter temperatures. Liao meant *calm*, considering most time was kept by the sun and the days got longer, the daily work could be spread out over more daylight hours and thus it had the potential to be less stressful than usual.

In that spirit, this month can be seen as a time to start bringing about change. Lean into the *Liao* feeling and enjoy the calm, creating it when you can't find it.

JUNE 1

Just because something might not be considered significant to others does not mean I need to lessen its value to me. This applies to my feelings, but also in the ways I choose to enjoy myself. My enjoyment is a worthwhile part of my self-care without the addition of outside opinions.

JUNE 2

The more value I place on my time, the more I will pay attention to what I invest that time in. By being aware of the areas that do not deserve the time they are getting, I can bring a more positive balance to my schedule overall.

JUNE 3

Success can be an important part of my life without taking away from my appreciation of the journey. Being able to love the process of life, and not only its destinations, will help me in the future by giving me a more enhanced appreciation of the goal itself. Success is not only about the result, it's mostly about the journey.

JUNE 4

Life is full of decisions and my happiness deserves to be considered when making those decisions. Sacrifice is needed at times, but it is not necessary for me to completely ignore the impact that my choices will have on my happiness. Being happy shouldn't be a deciding factor, but it should be in the conversation.

JUNE 5

It isn't always easy to make difficult decisions, but it does take courage to do so. I will start giving myself more credit when I show bravery in the face of life's challenges, instead of simply expecting myself to. Self-affirmation and appreciation will help create a strong foundation that will build my confidence and self-worth.

JUNE 6

The people who I consider role models should be in that position for a reason. I will be cognizant of the impact others' influence might have on me, including those I see as leaders. My respect is to be earned, and that includes those people who have authority roles in my life.

JUNE 7

The best things in life are found when I am willing to be patient and let it happen in its own time. There is wisdom in patience, and the more comfortable I become with that characteristic, the more I will appreciate what I gain in life.

JUNE 8

Being realistic is important, but so is having something larger than life to reach for. Having a dream to pursue brings an added sense of inspiration and purpose to my life. I will never let my life become one without a dream in it.

JUNE 9

Even though it can be difficult and conflicting at times, I recognize that honesty is one of the more vital characteristics that can be gained in life. I will make honesty a consistent priority, even when it makes a situation uncomfortable. Truth is worth more than my comfort in the long run.

JUNE 10

Just like there is no balance when I ignore my mental health, the same happens when I let my physical health slide. When I put effort into my own well-being and health, I am telling myself—and my insecurities—that I have worth in both mind and body. A healthy mind in a healthy body is what makes me complete.

JUNE 11

I am learning to take responsibility in my life, and that includes understanding what I do or don't do and the reasons for my actions or inactions contribute to my positive or negative habits. When I realize the importance of taking responsibility, I will see the need to put thought into each choice I make, regardless of how significant I consider it.

JUNE 12

Life is not meant to be spent avoiding interactions or assistance from others. While there can be positives in doing something on my own, there is nothing gained in not accepting help from those in my life. Allowing myself to be a part of a community will help me succeed, not weaken me because I need others. And others need me.

JUNE 13

There is great joy and benefit found in having the support of others, but at the end of the day, the most important thing is that I believe in myself. By building a foundation based on a belief that I can succeed, future conflicts and challenges will not take away that belief.

JUNE 14

There is nothing wrong with me having ambition. I am allowed to want better for myself and my loved ones and put in the work needed to get there, all free from outside negative influences and judgments. With focus, determination, and ambition on my side, I am giving myself the best chance to succeed consistently.

JUNE 15

An important part of my self-care is identifying areas in my life that are sources of negativity. When I am real about what those areas are, I can change them, even if it is difficult and may create conflict. Without first removing the negative, I cannot fully increase the positive.

JUNE 16

It isn't enough for me to just learn things that need to be changed I have to take action. Awareness is the first step, and I am committed to not just identifying but also doing what is needed for my present self improvement and for my future self.

JUNE 17

Being empathetic is an admirable trait, but I need to recognize the difficulties as well. True empathy means seeing things as another would, and even though that isn't always easy, I will use that characteristic to improve. I can become a better friend, partner, and person if I am willing to see what empathy wants to show me.

JUNE 18

When it comes to my creativity, I will learn when my expectations are needed and when they are not. There is value in creativity without a goal other than enjoyment and finding peace. The more I understand this, the more I can get from my creative moments.

JUNE 19

The more I see time as a guideline and not an absolute, the less stress I will have when managing it. Even though I know it isn't easy, when I can live more flexibly, I will have a clearer picture of how my time should be divided.

JUNE 20

When I wait and hope for inspiration to come, I am not setting myself up for success. However, when I work towards the drive and put effort into myself during the process, I will not only be able to seek success but also know how to handle it when I reach it.

JUNE 21

I am a unique individual, and because of that, I receive love in my own way. It is my responsibility, though, to be aware of my preferred method and see enough worth in myself to express it. By understanding this in myself, I can aim to love others as they prefer as well.

JUNE 22

In life, the happiness I bring to myself is just as important as the happiness I can bring to others. When I limit myself in any capacity, one way or the other, I am also limiting the ability I have to enjoy life, and appreciate the joy in others.

JUNE 23

It takes a courageous heart to take on a challenge, but it takes one braver still to pick myself up after a failed attempt and try again. As long as I get back up, I will never truly fail.

JUNE 24

Success is built on both a grasp of reality and the ability to imagine. When I see less value in my imagination regarding my success, I am limiting myself. To truly achieve what I set out to, it will take reality and imagination together.

JUNE 25

In my life, it is vital for the areas where I invest my loyalty to have worth and substance. As long as I remain aware and diligent, loyalty is a wonderful attribute for me to grow. I am also working to be aware of the difference between loyalty and obligation and act accordingly.

JUNE 26

I am the leader of my destiny. And being a leader does not only mean one thing, it requires a wide array of characteristics. To be the best leader I can be, I need compassion, patience, and a willingness to learn about the things I do not know yet.

JUNE 27

The more of a desire I have to speed up a process, the more I need to strengthen not only my resolve but also my patience. When something is truly worth having, it is worth the time it takes me to get there. I will remind myself when things get difficult that those characteristics come into play the most when I need to be steadfast.

JUNE 28

When I keep myself open to new experiences and new perspectives, I am giving my worldview a chance to grow. An open mind is the best way for me to experience all of the world instead of resigning myself to an isolated view.

JUNE 29

A key part of my success is remaining humble, no matter what happens. It is easy to get caught up in succeeding, but I recognize how important it is to act in a spirit of humility. It is possible to be proud of myself without it becoming a negative trait.

JUNE 30

The different things I want to achieve are valuable, and worth taking the time to see whether they can happen. Simply because something seems out of reach or challenging does not mean it is not worth the effort to pursue.

Monthly Reflections

What did this last month mean to me?

What daily inspiration had the most meaning to me?

This month I learned...

Chapter Seven: July

July got its name from one of the more ambitious figures in history, despite the tragic ending; Julius Caesar. It wasn't just because of his power or political influence, although that is a common understanding. Julio Caesar was actually the one who made some changes to the calendar created by the Romans, which led to the same one we are still using. Somehow, despite that impressive contribution to modern record keeping, most remember Caesar for something else entirely. What do you want to be remembered for?

This month is a good time to remind ourselves that everyone has a place in history, whether it is creating a calendar that lasts for 2,000 years or something else entirely, as long as it is personal and meaningful, your legacy can be whatever you want to make it.

JULY 1

I have a choice between being honest about what will help me achieve my goals and wanting something else to help instead. The right path to actually finding success doesn't always have to go the way I want to get me there. I will have faith that if I am honest with myself, I will reach my goals.

JULY 2

My health is about much more than just me. It is about taking care of myself to be there for those I love. It is about setting a good example for those who look up to me. It is about showing myself daily that I matter. By making my health a priority, I can do all this and more.

JULY 3

It is important for me to see repetition as building a solid foundation for a future habit. At my work, at home, or socially; reminding myself of this will help me avoid seeing it as mundane and view it as a positive, productive path. A path that will take me to my happy place.

JULY 4

When I see each interaction I have throughout the day as a new chance to positively affect someone, I will have a firm grasp on true compassion. It takes nothing away from me to be kind to someone else, so I will strive to see things through that lens.

JULY 5

I will work to bring organization into my life without being frustrated by the process. The more organized my life can be—in a way that is productive for me—the easier I can move forward feeling confident I am headed in the right direction. The effort is worth the result. I am capable of putting in the effort even when it is challenging.

JULY 6

There is nothing wrong with evaluating my work situation when I feel it is needed. When I get uncomfortable examining where I am I need to recognize the signal that a change might be needed. When I am aware of how I honestly feel about my profession and its impact on me, the more I can make positive choices for my future.

JULY 7

The way I react to my self-care is signaling one of two things to me. Either I prioritize myself and am willing to make time for self-care, or I see other things as more worthwhile and put my self-care lower on the list. The more I lean one way or the other, the more I strengthen that view. It is my responsibility to make self-care something important in my life.

JULY 8

When life's challenges knock me down, I have the option of seeing it as a disappointment or a chance to gain more experience. In life, I learn when I am willing to see mistakes as something necessary and, in the long run, positive. When I am open to falling a few times, I will set my fear aside and choose to learn instead.

JULY 9

The more I am able to see from someone else's perspective, the more overall understanding I will gain of myself. Empathy teaches compassion, and from that, I will be able to forgive, relate to, and love myself and others more. I am worth that effort.

JULY 10

Whether I realize it or not, the ways I choose to divide my time end up telling me where to direct my energy and focus. This thought might not be in line with my true self and the values I hold. Outside of my obligations, I have choices as to where my time goes, and those areas are where my focus and attention should be as well. By understanding the importance of where I place that attention, I will be discerning about the investment of energy it has the potential to be.

JULY 11

I understand that there will be times when I find inspiration naturally and times when I will be more responsible for cultivating it through my drive and ambition. I mustn't get complacent with either one. Either way, I have a role in the outcome, so I always have a hand in it no matter what.

JULY 12

Just like the food I eat, the content I decide to let into my mind will have an impact on me. It is important for me to take responsibility for what I view and listen to, even when it is simply entertainment. The final say is always up to me, but without taking the time to examine it, that is too big a risk to leave to chance. The health of my mind is at stake.

JULY 13

There are many different ways in which I can be happy and how I show it. It is not just about smiling and outward displays, it is about how I feel inside. My happiness can be quiet contentment in the now, or in a belief for a better future. When I do not confine myself to one definition, I am able to experience a full range of happiness instead of being disappointed with a limited version.

JULY 14

Peer pressure doesn't end after my teenage years, it just changes form. The more focused I am on how others see me, the more stock I will put into their opinions. However, when I get my worth from how I view myself, the external influences have very little power over me.

JULY 15

The more I am open to experiencing through my mind and imagination, the more I can remove the limits of the usual and common. When imagining is as much a part of the way I process the world around me, I become unburdened by the possible and extend my soul to reach my lofty dreams.

JULY 16

It is not realistic to expect life to never knock me down or for me to not fail. The important thing is the resilience I am able to show in the face of those missteps. As long as I understand that falling down isn't an ending, I will always have the strength to rise back up and move forward.

JULY 17

It is okay to have parts of my life without a specific and intended purpose; they can just exist because I like them. There is room in my life for both the necessary and the fun all at once. By seeing the value in both, I am permitting myself to include frivolity here and there.

JULY 18

The most effective tool I have is awareness. When I am truly aware, I can make better, more informed choices, see where change needs to occur, and recognize the small indicators that can be easily missed in the shuffle. I will continue to work on my awareness and keep it a priority.

JULY 19

Patience plays many parts in life, but the most important role is when I need to be patient with myself. It isn't always easy when mistakes occur and setbacks happen. Having the ability to be patient with my progress and the person I am despite those issues makes all the difference. The occurrences that could derail this journey of mine becomes a reminder of what is important in my life.

JULY 20

When I have an open mind as I go through life, I learn instead of judging, love instead of hating, and understand instead of demeaning. Having a willingness to understand others means creating a life that has a great capacity for love. The more committed I am to keeping that open mind, the more of life I will experience.

JULY 21

No matter how much I accomplish or what I achieve, being humble enables me to find success without losing the person I truly am. The more consistent I am with making room for humility in my life, the more opportunities for success I am opening myself up to. Humility doesn't only give perspective, it lets me remember why I put in the work and effort in the first place.

JULY 22

One way or another, everything in life comes down to perspective. What I see is not what someone else sees, but that doesn't mean someone has to be right or wrong. When I am able to understand and empathize with someone else's views, I will bring a more complete vision to my life.

JULY 23

I will not let myself be confined by only what is logical and considered probable. The realistic plans I have for my future matter just as much as my dreams do. One without the other leads to an imbalance in the future. My life should consist of the freedom to reach for the goals I desire, while also respecting the realities that come with it.

JULY 24

It can seem easier for me to tell a friend what I think they want to hear, but the truth is that honesty in those intense, vital moments will be more impactful. Telling someone what they might not like is never easy, but I am going to continue working on myself so I can put their well-being first and let honesty lead me in those situations.

JULY 25

While my life may not be all successes, in the moments where I did not succeed, I will strive to still find hope. It is hope that fuels my belief that I will succeed. Because life brings with it inevitable errors, without hope I cannot expect to move forward and truly accomplish what I desire.

JULY 26

My success relies on my ability to work and excel as it does on my willingness to rest when necessary. When I can accept rest with a positive attitude, I will be able to find refreshment even in the midst of busy times. The sooner I see rest as necessary, the easier I can incorporate it further into my routine.

JULY 27

Life is too big for me to not try new things. When I am willing to expand my horizons, I am opening myself up to not only new experiences, but new perspectives within those experiences. As I move forward, I will commit myself to being aware of those opportunities and not shying away from them when they arrive.

JULY 28

My mind is not an inanimate object that requires no further attention. Like a plant, if I put no effort into strengthening my mind, then the opposite will happen and it will weaken. Whether they are activities, learning tools, or any other action intended to maintain my mind, the bottom line is that the worst thing I can do for my mind is assume it does not need attention.

JULY 29

I must never forget that I gain nothing from an insistence on always being right. The more comfortable I get at admitting I was wrong, the more open I will be to the lessons that come afterwards. Mistakes are a part of life, but learning from them is not a guarantee. It is worth more to learn for the future than to be hard-headed for something I know isn't right.

JULY 30

By using uplifting words to describe myself, accepting compliments instead of shrugging them off, and having a positive outlook, I am building my self-esteem. I will not let the small things take away from the positive self image I am building for myself.

JULY 31

It isn't only what I schedule my time for that shows my priorities, because the things that I make time for—in spite of a schedule—truly shows where I am willing to invest passion and efforts. By being aware of those situations, I can identify those areas where I put more priority, possibly without realizing it, and to make improvements where they are needed.

Monthly Reflections

What did this last month mean to me?

What daily inspiration had the most meaning to me?

This month I learned...

Chapter Eight: August

What one person sees in their life isn't going to match up with another's view, and yet we live in a world where both can exist at the same time. The month of August is the perfect time to move forward in a spirit of understanding and acceptance, even if something seems different or you may not understand. As the Northern Hemisphere is using August to prepare for winter and wind down the hot summer temperatures, in the Southern Hemisphere they are leaving what would feel like *February*. Two very different experiences happening at the same time; no better example to use for these next 31 days.

While your hemisphere is experiencing August, what about the people around you? Those you love? This month can be a wonderful reminder to look through someone else's eyes, because when you understand someone, you can love and appreciate them in a way unique to who they are as an individual.

AUGUST 1

There will be days that are harder than others for me; that is not something I can control. What I do have control over, though, is how I choose to face it. I will be courageous in the face of a lack of desire to take action. Remaining stagnant is easy, showing courage in difficulty is not easy, but it is always worth it.

AUGUST 2

I am only held back by the limitations I put on my mind. If I can find out my self-imposed limitations, I can work towards repairing or removing them. The more aware I become of this, the more energy I can conserve by not confining myself. I am striving to realize the power I have in my thoughts and mind, and the benefit it can bring me.

AUGUST 3

I recognize that life will not do the work for me. Opportunities will present themselves, but it is up to me to take advantage of them. I will begin taking more responsibility for the chances I do and do not take. By being more aware of the opportunities that arise, I give myself a greater chance at succeeding.

AUGUST 4

I cannot promise myself that nothing bad will happen, but I can promise that I will be stronger in those times. When I stop trying to avoid the inevitable and instead prepare to weather the storm, I will grow and learn more than I ever have before.

AUGUST 5

My awareness is not only for recognizing and identifying the negatives in life, I also need to notice the positives. There is nothing wrong with acknowledging the good things in my life. By giving attention to the joys as well as the challenges I am cultivating a more balanced, more aware way of living that will only benefit me from here on out.

AUGUST 6

The best defense I have against unwise decisions and rash choices is patience. My patience can help in the long term, but I am also able to utilize that characteristic to avoid rushed situations. Sometimes all I need is a few moments to think before deciding, and being confident in my patience goes a long way to giving me those few moments.

AUGUST 7

The more I am able to not only see someone else's perspective, but view their solutions as viable to my situations, the more open-minded I can be. Putting aside my personal bias and ego in order to get a more full view on the matter will never be the wrong choice to make. Being consistent in doing so will make me wiser.

AUGUST 8

The less reliant I am on the approval of others, the more fulfilled I will allow myself to be. Whether it is my work, creatively, or socially, I am capable of affirming myself. With an approach based on my own approval, I can have a clearer understanding of what I need and want in life.

AUGUST 9

When I feel overwhelmed by life and underwater, that is when I need to have confidence in my perspective. I have power over my situation when I can pause and step back to see everything from a bigger picture view. Having perspective, especially in those moments, can make all the difference.

AUGUST 10

The time I have is not infinite, so the places I choose to dedicate myself to matter a great deal. I am not obligated to give my time anywhere. By doing this, I am making my time a priority, thus giving me another chance to strengthen my self worth. If my time is a priority, then I am a priority as well.

AUGUST 11

The honesty I share with myself is only going to make an impact if I also follow through. I cannot expect honesty to work alone, because without action, it is an unfinished project. When I see what needs to be changed, thanks to my honesty, then I also need to do something about that change. The more I follow through, the more power my honesty will have.

AUGUST 12

Hope is like a friend who is still there when everyone else is gone. I need to take a positive approach when it comes to hope because, when everything seems to be crashing down, hope is there for me. I will not see hope as a frivolity, because it holds the real power in my life.

AUGUST 13

All the work in the world will do me no good if I do not also see the value in rest. My goal needs to be longevity instead of simply trying to get through something. When rest becomes a regular part of my routine instead of an extra part to be crowbarred in, I will see my quality of work rise as well.

AUGUST 14

The further I am willing to look outside my own life, the richer my experience will become. The assumed safety of isolation is not comparable with the vast wealth of life that is to be found in the perspectives of others. Even though it might be hard at times, I will see the power in looking beyond my horizons and value the experiences of others that I can learn from.

AUGUST 15

The accomplishments in my life are significant to me and deserve to be recognized. When I can be affirming to myself regarding the things I achieve, I will be able to find fulfillment without the need for outside influence. While there is nothing wrong with desiring it from others, there is no replacement for being my own source of uplifting energy.

AUGUST 16

The building blocks of my life are the habits I keep. By examining the results I am getting and what I desire, I can be more aware of the kind of habits I should be forming and the ones that need to be removed or adjusted. When I make my habits a focus, I will be making a very positive step towards a balanced, healthy life in body and mind.

AUGUST 17

The steps I need to be taking to cultivate a positive self image should be done without judgement—from myself or others. Having good self-esteem is worth striving for, but I need to be my own biggest fan in those situations. I cannot be working towards my self image and also be fighting negativity within myself.

AUGUST 18

I will no longer allow myself to feel forced to have certain relationships in my life. The more distance I put between the people in my life and a feeling of obligation, the more sincere my relationships will be. Until I am honest and comfortable about those I choose to have in my life, I cannot be truly vulnerable with them.

AUGUST 19

I may not realize it, but the belief I have in the people I love matters a great deal to them. By understanding that impact and influence I can have in another's life, I will also understand the responsibility it brings. I will respect the privilege of having a say in someone's life and strive to uplift those I love just as I would want to be uplifted.

AUGUST 20

The places within myself that I choose to focus on is where I will see the deepest growth. Whether it is attention to a negative trait that needs improvement, or focusing on a loving characteristic, where I invest myself is where I will excel. This is why my awareness is so important to me, because focus in general is wonderful, but when I know where to focus I will be efficiently working towards my well-being in a specific manner.

AUGUST 21

I will work to be more aware of the difference between a job and a career. This is important because it will help me choose where to invest my energy. A job is short term and must be seen as temporary and a rung to something bigger and better. A career, however, is a long-term investment that will require a different level of patience and effort. Seeing the difference means I can plan and prepare wisely for my future.

AUGUST 22

My self-care needs to be based on the unique, individual needs that I have determined from my awareness, not based on what I want it to look like. I need to avoid the pressure to appear a certain way when it involves making unnecessary and damaging changes to my routine. Self-care is about what I need, not about optics or appearances. The deeper of an understanding I have about that, the more effective my self-care can be.

AUGUST 23

I will not let myself reach a point where I feel like I have nothing left to learn. My life is an ever-changing, flexible journey and the more open I remain to learning, the better chance of success I give myself. By setting aside pride and ego, I will discover new depths of myself and lessons I never considered before.

AUGUST 24

If I am truly seeking to live a loving life, it is imperative that I incorporate empathy into every aspect of it. Empathy will help me live beyond just myself, to never assume my view is the only one, and to appreciate the experiences and views of those around me. In order to love fully and completely, I must be able to live with a consistent attitude of empathy.

AUGUST 25

It is possible for me to live with a focused, solid work ethic and to live creatively as well. I do not need to box myself into just one thing or another. I am fully capable of finding fulfillment in both aspects of my life without having to set aside expression and creativity to find it.

AUGUST 26

Many problems in my life are avoidable if I learn to prepare and plan well. While I cannot avoid all of the curves in life, with focus on organization and a healthy sense of time management, I can live with a sense of preparedness instead of reactivity and anxiety.

AUGUST 27

My ambition is not something to stifle or hide. Instead, I will learn to listen to what it is telling me to plan for. When I am aware of the signals I get from my ambition, I can navigate the journey to accomplish what I set out to do. I will not let my drive be something negative, instead I will cultivate it and incorporate it into the road of life I am on.

AUGUST 28

When reacting to a situation, I always have a choice; act out of impulse, or act out of rationality. I will move forward with the intent to trust my mind, despite what may be going on in my life. Choosing a positive and rational reaction will make an impact, not just on the other person, but in my life as well. The more I make that decision, the more I will feel comfortable doing so until it is natural to me.

AUGUST 29

Even though it may seem simple, I am allowed to have things in my life just because they make me happy. I do not need to feel like I have to justify those things to myself. The more I see happiness as something of value and a need in life, the more I will make it a regular part of my efforts.

AUGUST 30

The goals I want to accomplish will not just work themselves out. I will act with courage when action is needed. I recognize the work it will take, and I also acknowledge that I am fully capable of taking on what life brings with an attitude of bravery. The things that are truly meaningful to me are worth fighting for.

AUGUST 31

The attitude with which I approach things matters a great deal. By choosing to have a positive approach I am setting the stage for productive growth to happen. I will put in the work so that I can keep negativity away from the things I am seeking to achieve. A positive environment is where true progress happens.

Monthly Reflections

What did this last month mean to me?

_____

_____

_____

_____

What daily inspiration had the most meaning to me?

_____

_____

_____

_____

This month I learned...

_____

_____

_____

_____

Chapter Nine: September

This month is a symbol for new beginnings, even later in life, or when we aren't expecting it. Autumn starts in the Northern Hemisphere while Spring is beginning in the Southern Hemisphere. Across the world, this is a chance for everything to balance itself out and prepare to move forward.

What will your beginning be this month? With all the attention given to New Year's resolutions, we often forget that fresh starts can happen at any time. What needs repairing or adjusting in your life? How will you use this to jumpstart goals you may have not thought of for some time? The possibilities are all there, it's up to you to decide which beginning will start today.

SEPTEMBER 1

The only way my dreams can be limited is when my imagination is limited as well. There is power in understanding that imagining something is the first step to making it happen. The bigger I am able to dream, the more I will be able to accomplish. I will work to avoid limiting myself and to use my imagination freely.

SEPTEMBER 2

With the right perspective and attitude, anything in my life can be an opportunity. Whether I succeed or fail, there are lessons to be learned in the experience. By putting in the effort to live with that spirit of opportunity, I will be able to learn no matter what happens.

SEPTEMBER 3

Being truly resilient means understanding myself enough to know how to recover from a misstep. While it is important to get back up and push forward, there is also wisdom in ensuring I am ready to get back up. Putting my well-being over expediency sets a precedent for a healthy future.

SEPTEMBER 4

There is a season for everything in my life, and knowing when to move on to the next one is an important trait to have. My awareness enables me to be sensitive to the growth and possibilities in each phase of life, and when to choose the next step up.

SEPTEMBER 5

There is a huge difference between what I want and what I need, but both of those need to come in their own time. When I can practice self-control despite a real desire to speed up the process to get what I want, it will be because I invested time in reflection and honesty about the situation. I cannot lean one way or the other, both my wants and needs have to be approached with a different mindset about what truly matters to me.

SEPTEMBER 6

I will make a real effort to react differently when I hear something I do not agree with. Instead of being impulsive or acting purely out of emotion, I will pause and try to see it from an alternate perspective than mine. I might not always end up changing my mind, but it is worth putting in the effort because when I am able to see from someone else's perspective, it will bring me growth and progress.

SEPTEMBER 7

Being open to change means a willingness to accept that I might not be right. I recognize the difference between being stubborn and actually taking the time to see if I am right. As difficult as it may be at times, I will work to bring a spirit of humility to those situations.

SEPTEMBER 8

Rather than being frustrated by things I do not know or things I have trouble learning, I will put worth in the perspectives of others to complete those gaps. Knowledge is not a one-player scenario, so the more viewpoints I welcome to my own perspective, the more varied and strong it becomes.

SEPTEMBER 9

There is nothing to be gained in making myself believe something is going well. I will stop putting my short-term comfort over my long-term well-being. When I am willing to be honest with myself from the beginning, I can avoid acting from the wrong beliefs.

SEPTEMBER 10

I cannot underestimate the power I have over my circumstances. The attitude and spirit I bring to each situation has a real influence on the result. By believing in hope instead of bringing a hopeless attitude, even to challenging situations, I am putting my inner power in the positive to come through.

SEPTEMBER 11

A vital part about knowing myself intimately is trusting when I need to put more effort in or when I need to pause and breathe. When this decision is based on what I need instead of an external demand, I can make the best choice for myself.

SEPTEMBER 12

The unknown will no longer be a place of fear for me. I am capable and strong. The unknown is indeed a place of opportunity. I will put my focus and energy in my ability to adapt and learn, so that I can take on things that used to frighten me. The power to turn the unknown into the understood lies with me and I accept the responsibility. Learning and adapting are a part of my evolution.

SEPTEMBER 13

While I am aware of the people who mean a great deal to me and have influence in my life, that does not always mean that they are aware of it. I am determined to show recognition to those who have helped in my life. I will also work to become more comfortable in expressing that recognition in the future.

SEPTEMBER 14

My positive habits are not the only ones that should get attention. It is my responsibility to not let my negative habits slide either, even if I don't consider them a priority. Any habit that is in my life will influence who I am and what I can achieve or not. So the more attentive I am, the more improvement I can bring into my life.

SEPTEMBER 15

Having a positive self-image does not mean skewing the truth for my benefit. If I am not honest about myself, I will just be setting myself up for disappointment later on. When I am able to have an honest relationship with myself about who I truly am, I will not be influenced by what anyone thinks of me.

SEPTEMBER 16

Setting a goal is the first step, but if I do not believe that I can achieve it, I am not setting myself up for success. I need to begin with a foundation of belief in myself, because only then will I be able to invest all of myself into the endeavor.

SEPTEMBER 17

I cannot succeed if my focus is only set on the long term or the short term. It will require being focused on both of those times in order for me to be truly successful. I will see both long and short term as equally important, and put forth effort in both instead of continuing to be out of balance.

SEPTEMBER 18

Being invested in my self-care means being willing to pull away when it is detrimental to my growth. This means with people, jobs, or anything that demands my attention and consumes my energy. By recognizing the positives in taking time for myself and my benefit, I will become more comfortable in making decisions based on its impact on me rather than solely on others.

SEPTEMBER 19

The freedom found in creating and expressing cannot be undervalued. I recognize that an outlet for creativity or expression in general is imperative to a healthy, well-rounded life. My creativity allows me to view and solve problems more openly and with added innovation. The details hardly end up mattering, but when I take time and focus solely on creativity, I am telling myself that I am worth this investment.

SEPTEMBER 20

Because there is no singular solution to managing my time, I will work to develop a method that works for my individual situation and priorities. By focusing on my needs instead of my wants or what others need or want, I am being true to what I actually benefit from.

SEPTEMBER 21

It is important to understand what drives me. The more I am aware of my drive and what helps me accomplish things, the better prepared I will be for those situations. I can better navigate the journey when I understand what would assist or hinder me.

SEPTEMBER 22

One of the best practices I can adopt is that of being selfless. When I am able to put others first I am teaching myself that it is important to focus on things outside myself. By seeing past the typical self-centered views of society, I can impact people on a very real level.

SEPTEMBER 23

Even though I recognize that it is difficult to show positivity in hard situations, I also realize the overwhelming benefit in staying focused on the positive. When I choose to react from a positive mindset over the option requiring less effort, I am forming a habit. So the times after that, it will progressively become easier for me to choose correctly.

SEPTEMBER 24

It is far too easy for me to pass by the wonderful things in my life and not be grateful. I will learn to move forward in a spirit of gratitude for what I am blessed with. I am willing to put in the effort so that I do not forget to be grateful when good things happen.

SEPTEMBER 25

I will keep myself open to discovery. The world is far too big for me to become stagnant, so I welcome the chance to discover new things. Whether it is relationships, opportunities, or just a form of enjoyment, it is worth pursuing.

SEPTEMBER 26

Life is all about chances. If I do not keep myself open to the opportunities that come around, I may not get another shot. Using my awareness, I will be able to recognize when those chances arise. Even when they don't all work out, it is worth putting the effort into the opportunity.

SEPTEMBER 27

I am working to recognize the difference between knowledge and wisdom, but I also recognize the value in both. I need knowledge to be informed about my decisions, but wisdom is what shows me the direction that is right for me. If I only have one or the other then I will only be giving half the effort I am capable of.

SEPTEMBER 28

The drive to succeed is not in itself a negative quality, but when it gets mixed up with my pride and ego, it can become a detriment. I understand the importance of being a driven person while also coming from a place of humility.

SEPTEMBER 29

Empathy doesn't end when I know what someone thinks. It means taking the time to understand why they think that as well. The more I am able to truly see from someone else's perspective, the more depth of understanding I can have of their experience. I will also have a clearer view of what they have to offer to the world.

SEPTEMBER 30

Being positive does not mean having an unrealistic view of life, it just means making the effort to look deeper. I can find the positives when I try to, it just means that I need to set aside my desire to react a certain way and instead choose to see the possibilities and believe in myself.

Monthly Reflections

What did this last month mean to me?

What daily inspiration had the most meaning to me?

This month I learned...

Chapter Ten: October

This month can be seen as a time of transition; when the hot weather has cooled and the preparations for the colder season begins. This transitional feeling exists no matter where you are on earth. While the winter season is just around the corner in the Northern Hemisphere, in the Southern Hemisphere the preparations are for Spring to arrive instead.

No matter where you are, you can still use this month as a time to gear up for the last portion of the year. It can be stressful thinking about possible upcoming holidays, work deadlines, or school exams. While all those looming events can seem overwhelming, that is the perfect time to bring some more affirmation to your life. Building a positive attitude and developing a proactive approach towards your life will not only make excellent use of a time usually spent worrying, but when those times arrive, you will be ready and able to enjoy them.

OCTOBER 1

I have a choice between living in worry and deciding to actually deal with my worries. I will work at recognizing that just living in worry does not ease my challenges. Deciding to be prepared and to act on those challenges does put me in a better place to constructively handle those situations. Acting on what I can control is key. The time and effort ahead of time are well worth it for the result.

OCTOBER 2

My life may have difficulties, but it is not set against me. When these difficulties arise, it is not wanting me to fail, it is an opportunity to learn from the experience. It won't be easy, but I can begin changing my perspective on this, so I recognize the possibilities instead of fearing the challenge. Things don't happen to me, they happen for me.

OCTOBER 3

The real threat to my progress isn't the unexpected things life throws at me, it is the times of inaction. When I allow stagnancy into my life it erodes my momentum and can lead to denial regarding the danger of giving in to that sense of comfort. By actively avoiding these times of being stagnant I will not miss out on progress and opportunities.

OCTOBER 4

I must not let myself get too focused only on how my actions impact my present self, because that action will also affect myself in the future. By not only seeing that balance, but putting effort into keeping it, I will not only be making responsible choices in the now, but ensuring it sets my future self up for success as well.

OCTOBER 5

A part of life is that things change, and what inspires me is not immune to those changes. In order for me to give myself the best chance for success, I need to be open towards those shifting drives. Just because the things that spark my ambition change throughout my life, it does not mean that the inspiration is any less than it was before.

OCTOBER 6

I will learn to stop wasting energy on only imagining what would make me happy, and begin working at making it a reality instead. The things that make me happy are worthwhile enough to not just exist in my mind. By putting in this effort, I will be proving to myself that my pursuit of happiness is important enough.

OCTOBER 7

The positive changes I want to bring to my life will not always come about easily. I need to recognize this and understand that the courage it will require doesn't mean I have to be fearless. It means that when I am afraid or worried, I can push forward in spite of it; that is what my courage can do.

OCTOBER 8

In those times when nothing seems to be working for me, my best weapon to help me rise above the difficulty is positivity. It will not fix everything, but positivity is the first step to dealing with difficult times. I must not discount the impact that I can achieve by bringing a different, positive perspective to a situation. By keeping this in mind and close at hand, I will be ready when it is needed—even unexpectedly.

OCTOBER 9

I can bridge the gap between a desire and reality by picturing what outcome I would like and how this would translate into my life. This is an important step for my preparedness, and can help focus my efforts now on what really matters. By imagining how I want it to go will influence how I navigate the situation.

OCTOBER 10

My life is not defined by the times that challenge me or that even defeat me, but rather for how I responded to them. My resilience to respond is a strength that I cannot take for granted. By knowing where my strengths are and how to implement them, I can be steadfast when I am challenged.

OCTOBER 11

Being aware of the negatives in my life that need to be amended is productive, but it is just as important for my awareness to recognize the positive choices I make as well. The negatives can teach me, but without affirming myself for the correct actions as well, the process is incomplete and unfair to myself.

OCTOBER 12

My patience is not supposed to only extend to others, because it is just as impactful for me to be patient with myself. This will allow me to take the situations in my stride—both positive and negative. When I can be patient with myself I will give myself more opportunities to grow without judgment and to live without unnecessary stress.

OCTOBER 13

Having positive self-esteem does not mean that I never feel insecure or that I am always happy with myself. It means that I am always working to improve myself and the way I see who I am. I am on a journey that requires understanding as well as my effort, both of which must be done without judgment.

OCTOBER 14

When I think about the values I find most important in life, that is what I should look for in the people I choose to surround myself with. There is nothing wrong with being selective about who I allow to influence me or have access to my life. The relationships I have should be built on mutual respect of values and beliefs, not tolerance of the negative traits.

OCTOBER 15

When I try to force inspiration to come, I am simply creating friction. However, when I examine my time and use patience in implementing it I will find a much more organic result. Just because inspiration doesn't come or work at one point doesn't dictate that it isn't meant to be, I just need to allow it to flow instead of forcing it.

OCTOBER 16

When I find myself losing focus, the tendency to react in frustration only brings more difficulty to the situation. In those moments, the most important thing for me to remember is that patience is the tool and frustration is destructive. My focus is not served well from me getting frustrated, so by maintaining my self-control, I am giving myself a better chance to regain that focus.

OCTOBER 17

The areas of my life that I am dedicated to may not always be lined up with what is best for me. It is important that I take the time to discern whether something is worth the time I dedicate to it. By being more particular and not just investing my energy everywhere, I will be able to give more of myself to the areas that truly matter.

OCTOBER 18

When I am able to approach my life with complete honesty, it will allow me to see it in a much clearer way. It is through that honesty that I will be able to recognize where my energy has been wasted and where my effort should be directed towards. The more honesty I can bring to the situations in my life, the more purposeful and direct my actions will have the strength to be.

OCTOBER 19

I am not always able to deal with trying times in my life, but I can make sure that no matter how challenging things get I don't need to lose hope. Many things may be out of my control, but I am able to hold onto the hope that things will get better. But first I must act on the things that I have control over. Without both hope and action, I am not as strong as I could be.

OCTOBER 20

I need to begin seeing the benefit and progress made not only in times of action but also in periods of reflection. It is not halting my progress, instead, it gives me a greater chance of finding insights and new angles for how to improve. Progress doesn't just mean pushing forward, it also means knowing when the most beneficial thing I can do is to reflect.

OCTOBER 21

There are moments in my life that are uniquely special to me, and because of that, I must allow myself to give them recognition. When I can freely recognize the times that stand out, I will bring more motivation to my life. Outside motivation won't always be there, but when I can build myself up, I become less reliant on others for my self-image and worth.

OCTOBER 22

Life is full of learning opportunities, but they can easily be mistaken for roadblocks if I am not aware enough. When I respond patiently and in a discerning manner, I won't miss out when those chances come around. This will set my future up for more possibilities.

OCTOBER 23

Creativity has many applications in my life, including being able to see and think outside the box. By seeing my creative traits as a catalyst for future positive decisions, I am giving myself a better chance to work through problems. The more I work at enhancing that creativity, the more it will be a helpful tool in my life's productivity.

OCTOBER 24

When I do not understand something the best reaction I can have is deciding to learn more about it. The less time I spend focusing on the problem, the more energy and time I will have to formulate a solution. Information leads to more understanding, and that will help me avoid pitfalls like frustration and misplaced focus.

OCTOBER 25

There is a difference between comfort and the danger of losing momentum. I can give myself comforts without putting my productivity at risk, but I must avoid being quick to label one or the other. By being more analytical regarding this particular matter I can stop withholding comforts and still continue down a productive path.

OCTOBER 26

A key part of setting myself up for success is believing that it can happen. The confidence I have in my ability to accomplish a goal plays a huge role in the outcome. When I enter a situation with the attitude of accomplishing, plus the belief that I can do it, it goes a long way to achieving success.

OCTOBER 27

It is possible for me to be at my best in both my work and personal life without sacrificing one or the other, or risking burning myself out. By widening my focus to include both career and home, I can be more aware of the balance, or lack of it. The more balanced I am able to be in the main aspects of my life, the more capable I will be of bringing my fulfillment to each.

OCTOBER 28

While I grow from being challenged, those are not the only situations in which I can find personal growth. I need to dispel this stigma that deep growth and progress can only be found through difficulty. Life is filled with chances to grow that are not fraught with challenge, it just takes awareness and a willing perspective for me to recognize those as well as the usual rough times.

OCTOBER 29

I will be more proactive in recognizing when a situation is not a good or healthy fit, and when I should press forward in confidence. This knowledge only comes through my awareness of myself and understanding what result is more beneficial to me. When I am able to recognize where my skills and talents would be wisely used and a good fit, I will find that the places I put my effort are correct.

OCTOBER 30

Because I cannot avoid the low points in life, it is important for me to know what tools help lift me out of them. By being proactive and preparing for the less than ideal times, when they do occur, I will be able to care for myself during the low moment and also have help climbing out. I can remove the stress of unfounded shame that used to come from having those difficult times with myself, and from that, I give myself the freedom to work through the experience in a healthy way.

OCTOBER 31

Accomplishing a goal of mine is something significant, but the goal itself is not all that I should appreciate. I will learn more by seeing the value in the journey towards the goal just as much as the finish line itself. Without appreciating that portion of the process, I will not be as prepared for what I accomplish. A balanced approach with both areas—goal and journey—both appreciated means that I can do more with the results.

Monthly Reflections

What did this last month mean to me?

What daily inspiration had the most meaning to me?

This month I learned...

Chapter Eleven: November

This month is unique because it is a sort of reminder that the year is coming to a close. December tends to bring finality, but November has a more calm approach, like being told you have enough time to do everything in. It is in that spirit that this month's inspirations can be drawn. So much energy and time is spent worrying about there not being enough hours in the day—and days in a month, etc.—all the while those precious minutes are ticking by.

Instead of renewing that same cycle all over again, use this month to speak productivity and completion into the days instead of anxiety and trepidation. Many cultures have attributed this particular month to the transition into the elderly years—not as an ending, but a different kind of beginning. This is yet another way of being reminded that there is more time than many believe. Even when things seem like they are winding down, there are beginnings everywhere if they can just be found.

As November starts, enter with a sense of renewal, setting aside the rush and worry that usually corresponds with this time of the year. One more inspiration as the month begins: most people don't know that the entire month is set aside for *National Gratitude Month*, so rather than waiting for one day to be thankful, take time each day to look past the negatives and find a bit of gratitude amongst it all.

NOVEMBER 1

The more I invest my energy into worrying about time, the more time I am losing. I will work to improve my mindset so that instead of focusing on how much time I have or haven't got, I will use that energy wisely. As hard as it may be to remember, time passes the same whether I focus on it or not, so worrying does nothing to improve my situation. I will focus on my most important year-end tasks and will use my time effectively and efficiently on them.

NOVEMBER 2

There is a big difference between being productive and being constantly working or moving. Just because I am able to do something does not mean that it deserves my time and attention. When I start to see that quality matters far more than quantity, I will not only increase my productivity, but increase how satisfied I am with said progress as well.

NOVEMBER 3

Stepping outside of a comfort zone looks different for everyone, so I can't judge my experiences by what others have done (or not done). I can be adventurous and step outside of my comfort zone while still respecting my well-being and mental stability. While one person may enjoy skydiving, another finds the same rush in completing a puzzle; my life and experiences are mine to enjoy and define.

NOVEMBER 4

The way I see and approach a situation will have a large impact on how I can react to it. While it may be less effort to have a negative and passive view, the positive and proactive approach is much more effective at increasing my productivity and lessening the stress it has on me. The results will reflect the change in my attitude when I combine it with my work and effort.

NOVEMBER 5

I will not let my friendliness or helpfulness be taken advantage of (directly or indirectly). There is nothing wrong with setting boundaries in my life, and that includes informing others when those boundaries have been crossed. The way others react to my boundaries is not my responsibility, and I cannot allow their reaction to lessen my resilience. I will get comfortable with being uncomfortable, and it is okay that I ask for space.

NOVEMBER 6

Life moves very fast, and because of this it is all the more important for me to pause and express gratitude. This doesn't just mean when something momentous occurs, it is important for even the things that seem common to be recognized with gratitude. When I can be grateful and show thanks on every day, it will bring me a new depth of fulfillment and happiness for the life I have.

NOVEMBER 7

It does not take anything away from me to be kind. I do not know what others are going through in their lives, and that act of kindness might be just what they need. By keeping that positive mindset and recognizing others' experiences I will act in a way I would like others to act towards me, but without expectation.

NOVEMBER 8

Patience does not mean the need to tolerate things that are damaging to me. I will work to understand the line between what is tolerating and what is damaging so that I can maintain my patience without allowing negative results to occur because of it. When I can find the healthy limits to my patience I will be able to make smarter choices and be more aware of these limitations in the future

NOVEMBER 9

I am a talented person, and there is no reason why I should not be proud of what I am capable of. I will stop comparing myself to others and focus on the gifts I have and what I bring to the world. When I can see my talents free from judgment and comparisons, I will truly see what I can do and what I will be able to accomplish.

NOVEMBER 10

What I do when no one is looking is almost more important than what I do in the open. The standards I have for myself should be consistent across all aspects of my life, and the more difference I allow between the private and public self, the more difficulty I will create for myself. By creating a consistent self, I will also be creating more stability and potential for my future self. What defines my character is what I do when no one is watching.

NOVEMBER 11

Just like there is a season for everything, there is a time for action and effort, then a time to be more easygoing. Being more relaxed when the time allows is not a problem, it is a way of showing myself that my well-being matters and that I can achieve more results, even from unexpected places. Being able to pause and continue moving forward, but with more ease, will allow me to avoid burnout and create more opportunities for progress.

NOVEMBER 12

Learning comes in many forms, school being just one of them. There is no shame in admitting that I do not know something, but I also then need to take the next step and educate myself. The more comfortable I am with learning and finding out my blind spots consistently, the more knowledge I will allow myself to absorb. My self-education is not only important, it will lead to a better version of myself. The progress I can achieve will depend more on how I deal with not knowing than on anything I do know.

NOVEMBER 13

Understanding the differences between honesty, directness, and being overly critical of myself will be very helpful to me. The ability to speak truth and honesty without being careless with another's feelings is a valuable trait indeed. The more I am able to see from someone else's perspective, the more I will be able to give advice and speak truth into their lives without causing unnecessary damage or emotional pain.

NOVEMBER 14

My self-awareness is the key to putting my discipline into action with the most success. When I know the areas of my life that need to be focused on and the reasons to do so, I can avoid any confusion or stress. Understanding where my willpower struggles will give my self-discipline the best chance to help me work through a situation. If I am aware of my problem areas, I will be able to invest my energy wisely and find solutions with more ease.

NOVEMBER 15

I am on this earth to live, not just to exist. An excellent way for me to make sure of this is to live purposefully. When I take action with purpose, I will be creating a solid foundation for my future. The more sure I am about where I want to be and how I want to get there, the more efficient my progress can be.

NOVEMBER 16

There is nothing inherently inadequate about being curious, as long as a sense of awareness and reasoning is brought along as well. I will allow myself the freedom to be curious, rather than resist and vilify that curiosity. This will enhance my imagination, my creativity, and give me new perspectives on life that I previously hadn't considered. Removing the negative stigma from curiosity isn't only helpful, it broadens my world.

NOVEMBER 17

Because life is always changing, the more adaptable I am, the more stress I will be able to avoid. I cannot expect difficulty or challenges to never come up, so when they occur, it is my adaptability that will allow me to not just work through them, but grow as well. The more I work at adapting, the easier it will become and the more I will start to learn from the experience.

NOVEMBER 18

I am not giving myself the best chance to succeed unless I can recognize needs in both myself and in others. The balance in this particular area is paramount. Only focusing on one—me or them—sets me up for a lesser fulfillment every time. When I am able to see each situation as unique, and then determine how it impacts both myself and others will give me the best chance to make well-rounded, healthy decisions.

NOVEMBER 19

Productivity in the short term is an excellent goal, but I cannot forget the importance of playing the long game as well. While being productive in the short term can move things forward, when I am also bringing more long-term ideas into the mix I am focusing on my ultimate goal as well as the impact along the way. How something makes me or someone else feel can be just as important as the productivity level—both in the long and short term.

NOVEMBER 20

I am worthwhile, and because of this, the goals and dreams I have are valuable as well. Having this perspective will let me be ambitious without attaching any guilt or limitations to it. By viewing myself as someone worthy of success and happiness, I am giving myself permission to not just recognize my ambitions, but to pursue them as well. The things I want and aim for are important simply because they are mine.

NOVEMBER 21

Enthusiasm can mean different things to each person, while still maintaining its impact. I do not need to match anyone else's enthusiasm to show my own life and goals the support they deserve. When I remove the judgment from that picture, I will start to see a more open approach to the kind of enthusiasm I bring to life.

NOVEMBER 22

It is not my responsibility to make others feel comfortable when it takes precedence over my feelings. Life is full of good days and bad days, and I can experience both in the ways that fit my life. How someone else reacts to my feelings is theirs to deal with, and I will work at accepting that as a truth in my life. I am allowed to feel the way I feel.

NOVEMBER 23

I do not need to fabricate positive emotions in order for me to classify a day as "good". I can have different standards for each day, even when it means going easy on myself for the sake of my well-being. I am taking stress away from myself by also removing the need to classify the day; I can be happy without needing to qualify it.

NOVEMBER 24

There is room for me to be both trusting and cautious at the same time. Just like in the rest of my life, it comes down to balance. It is important to be trusting and vulnerable, but I recognize the importance of being wary about who or what situation gets that part of myself. By balancing both trust and caution, I can experience the fullness of life while still seeing my well-being and stability as a priority.

NOVEMBER 25

Just because something has been done before does not mean it isn't worthy of being appreciated. Regular appreciation—of both myself and others—will give me a more grateful perspective for life as a whole. By prioritizing appreciation over expectation as an important part of me, I am giving it the chance to have a positive impact on both myself and those in my life.

NOVEMBER 26

By truly listening to others, I will learn the benefit of patience and prioritizing others over myself. Knowing the difference between talking to people and listening to them is taking a real interest in what they say instead of waiting for my turn to speak. When I can make this kind of listening a regular part of who I am, I will see increases to my personal growth as well.

NOVEMBER 27

While there is nothing wrong with me expressing my emotions, there is value found in maintaining my temperance, especially in situations that rarely result in it. Because I know that life's challenges cannot be fully avoided, when they do occur, I can maintain control of the situation by not losing my composure. When I react in a stoic manner, I will find more and more that the challenging situations become manageable and solutions are more readily available. Temperance is a habit that can be developed.

NOVEMBER 28

If I choose to focus solely on the results of my endeavors, then I will be controlled by the outcome. However, if I decide to focus on the process rather than the outcome, I am able to take back control. There will be times when things do not go the way I would have liked, but by focusing on where my attention and energy go, I will be sharpening my discipline and focus towards the end-goal. My appreciation can determine the way I end up seeing an experience, so aiming it towards positive growth will give me the opportunity to find good among the bad.

NOVEMBER 29

My awareness doesn't only give me the best chance to make positive choices, it also allows me to be more specific in expressing myself. When I know why something bothers me, or why I enjoy something, I can express it better to both myself and others. This allows me to be a better friend, partner, and family member because I can tell others both what I am feeling and how best to help me. Every chance to increase my awareness is always time well spent.

NOVEMBER 30

My ability to manage my time truly comes down to how honest I am willing to be with myself. When I can allow that self-honesty to dictate how I prioritize my time, I will be able to do so without the worry that I am overwhelming myself or not doing enough. When my time-management is based on what is actually the best for me, I can be the best for both myself and others.

Monthly Reflections

What did this last month mean to me?

What daily inspiration had the most meaning to me?

This month I learned...

Chapter Twelve: December

January generally holds the air of a fresh start and renewal after a long year, but you can only discover that renewal after you have reflected over the events of the 300 days that have come before. That is where December comes in—because reflection is right in its wheelhouse.

No matter where on the globe you are—snow or warmer weather—the end of the year tends to bring a plethora of emotions into play and that can be a lot to handle at times. It can be far too easy for a period of peaceful reflection to become a stress-filled month instead. Rather than just anticipating the challenges and "pushing through", this is the chance to take back control of a time of year that can set the tone for the next phase of life.

This doesn't need to be a countdown, which it tends to be framed as, because again that puts way too much stress on an already strained time. Think of this as a great warm-up that will lead to a better, more productive coming year. Thirty-one more chances to inspire and build on the foundation that *you* have created and strengthened—not a bad way to write a close to what will just be one of many chapters in your life.

DECEMBER 1

My word should mean something; not just to others, but to myself as well. When I am sincere and transparent, it will display my true integrity. Investing my effort and focus on building my character is always a worthwhile use of my time.

DECEMBER 2

There are many aspects of my life that should be handled in a serious manner, but I cannot forget the importance of including humor. Whether it is in times of stress or difficulty, alleviating the intensity can work in my favor. When I see humor as a tool in my life rather than a luxury, I can improve my relationship with it and learn what role it plays for me.

DECEMBER 3

As stressful as my life can be, I need to remember that others are experiencing their own struggles as well. It does not take away from me when I show kindness and friendliness to another person. By recognizing that I can have a positive impact on someone else, I will be working on expanding my worldview and to see outside my own perspective.

DECEMBER 4

There is value in being a reliable person. By doing so, I am showing respect to others and their time, but I am also giving myself the opportunity to have other qualities to shine within me. By making the effort to be more reliable to others and myself, I will enhance both personal and professional relationships.

DECEMBER 5

When I am able to do things in the present that will benefit my future self, I will begin to live and act in more than just the "now". By prioritizing the future version of who I am, it helps me to consider the quality of the decisions I make now and how they will impact me down the road. This will help me with my patience and in how I prioritize in my life overall.

DECEMBER 6

When it comes to my productivity, stress is one of the biggest enemies of my forward progress. Because stress tends to manifest itself as distraction, when I am aware and prepared for the distractions, I will be giving my productivity the chance to succeed. The less stressed and less distracted I am, the more progress I will be able to make and the more productive my work will be.

DECEMBER 7

Life's challenges will never cease completely, so it is all the more important for me to be able to maintain a calm demeanor when those challenges arise. Challenges are not a negative in life, rather they are what allows me to grow, to gain experience, and to become a better version of myself. Rather than denial, I will be prepared and have a realistic approach when life's challenges occur. By keeping calm in those situations, I will be able to learn and grow from that challenge.

DECEMBER 8

Kindness is one of the most important and overlooked traits I can have, but not just towards others, towards myself as well. The way I treat and speak about myself has an impact on the self-image I maintain, so the kinder I can be, the more healthy that image can be. I am able to treat myself with kindness and still have a realistic view of life. By giving myself the freedom to change I am proving my worth to myself, and showing that I care about the person I am and who I am becoming.

DECEMBER 9

While it may be easier to slide into the negative habits I have, by investing my energy and focus on the positive habits in my life I will be giving priority to the healthier, happier side of myself. The negative habits deserve focus to be worked on, but too often the positives get lost in the mix. I am capable of seeing both types of habits, but I have control over how I approach each.

DECEMBER 10

Instead of struggling to create a work-life balance, I will start to strive for harmony. This means that I will not be controlled or overly influenced by the emotional roller coasters that come from trying to fully exist in both places. Harmony is about boundaries rather than struggling and stressing over balance.

DECEMBER 11

There is a huge benefit to being able to know how and what I need for my own self-care. I cannot ever see my awareness as anything but a positive, because it is through that awareness I can learn what truly refreshes and helps me reset. Because I know and accept that life will bring difficulties, knowing ahead of time what will allow me to maintain my path and pace through self-care and fortitude, I will be able to establish a positive mindset that will translate to good feelings and emotions for others around me.

DECEMBER 12

Creativity comes in a wide variety of forms, and because of this, it is important for me to explore where mine is. By discovering the details of my creativity, I will be able to channel life's stresses and challenges into something positive and productive. I will be accepting of my personal kind of creativity, and respect it as a vital piece of my well-being and stability.

DECEMBER 13

By recognizing the benefits of keeping a regular journal, I am giving myself another tool of self-reflection to help me not only improve myself, but understand myself better as well. This will give me a healthy outlet that I can rely on to be a safe space to vent and explore my thoughts. The effort spent in finding the journaling method that works for me is well worth the benefits that will come from it in the future.

DECEMBER 14

I need to be aware of my own negative tendencies so that I can avoid self-sabotaging. By being transparent with myself and addressing my struggles, I will end the destructive cycle of being ashamed and instead be able to focus on finding healthy outlets. The way I treat and speak about myself matters, so by acting in a positive way towards myself, I will stop self-sabotage before it can take root.

DECEMBER 15

My life is not determined by the troubles and struggles I have gone through, but rather in the responses I have had towards them. By recognizing that resilience is not a permanent state, but a way of growth, I can see my experiences through a more positive lens, and as a result, I can take some constructive steps to help myself. I am not defined by the negatives, because every life has them, but by my responses. Because with every situation and challenge I face, I prove to myself that I have the freedom to choose my reaction.

DECEMBER 16

It is absolutely worthwhile to be patient with others, but a commonly forgotten aspect of this is also being patient with myself. Whether this means reviewing my standards or being more understanding about what I have gone through, I deserve to show myself patience. When I see my life through that view of patience, I will be able to avoid being hard on myself when it is unnecessary and unproductive.

DECEMBER 17

The more honest I am with myself, the more growth I will have the chance to obtain. There is no long-term benefit found in being dishonest with myself. All it does is create a divide between what is reality and how I see things. It may not be easy, but the more consistent I am with my self-honesty, the more problem areas I will be able to recognize and start to repair.

DECEMBER 18

The experiences that I have gone through in life are an incredibly valuable source of wisdom for my future, if I reflect on them. Whether the situation worked out well or not, by acting in awareness, self-reflection, and transparency, I can look back and gain wisdom for the experiences that have yet to happen. When I can understand this and believe in the wisdom gained, I will have more help in the future.

DECEMBER 19

The way I react when someone else does something that does not work out will give a glimpse into how understanding of a person I am being at that moment. By seeing another's actions as though they were mine, I can bring more empathy into the situation. When I am able to temper my reaction and instead see it from another viewpoint, I can avoid a negative, swift response and instead act with understanding and kindness.

DECEMBER 20

When I give my full effort and attention to something, I have the ability to experience a flow state of mind that enhances my focus and abilities. The effort and time that I invest in getting to that flow state is worthwhile because from there my productivity and progress can reach new heights. By giving myself the chance to reach flow state I am showing myself another way in which I prioritize myself and my productivity.

DECEMBER 21

The true test of my willpower and discipline occurs when there is no immediate consequence other than my own view. By first recognizing a situation as significant, I can prepare and invest my energy in being self-disciplined. The more consistent I am in this, the stronger my willpower will become and the more confident I will be in my ability to be self-disciplined even when I am alone. To strengthen my willpower, I will begin recognizing the reasons for the decisions I make or fail to make. Any behavior that I am unaware of is much harder to manage.

DECEMBER 22

I am not perfect, and because of this, it means I have made mistakes in life and in the future I will not always make the correct choice. Knowing and accepting this, it is vital that I can show myself forgiveness for the times I did not choose wisely. I can hold myself accountable and learn from the mistakes, but the most important part of the process is being able to forgive myself. This may not be easy or quick, which is okay, because daily attention to this part of myself will end up being invaluable for a healthy, positive future.

DECEMBER 23

When I am able to accept and love my unique self, it will allow me the freedom to appreciate the originality that comes with it. Being different is rarely easy, but by truly seeing and understanding the person I am, I am showing the original part of me that it is welcomed, appreciated, and accepted.

DECEMBER 24

My awareness does not exist to help me recognize only the positive things in life, it becomes truly priceless when it alerts me to the negatives. Seeing the positive parts is important without a doubt, but it is only half the process without also seeing the negatives. I understand that both exist within me and in my life, so when I am aware of both the positives and negatives, I can respond well. I do this by accepting and taking joy in the positive, but also in exploring how to improve and repair the negatives.

DECEMBER 25

It takes confidence to overcome many things in life, but humility is what allows me to see past my pride and ego down to the truth. Even with excellent awareness, my mind can sugarcoat the issues, which avoids the difficulty of seeing it but also removes the chance to bring change. When I can set aside what I want and aim for what I need, I will be able to strengthen my humility as well as my view of reality.

DECEMBER 26

It can be very easy to see all the difficulties, negatives, and issues that may arise in the future, but unless it is also tempered with hope, it will only bring me stress. It is important to be prepared for what will come as long as there is no despair involved. Hope is not setting myself up for disappointment, it gives me the freedom to believe that I can succeed and accomplish what I set out to do.

DECEMBER 27

In the bustle and complexities of life it can be far too easy to have things slip my mind. This is why it is so important for me to remember the relationships in my life that are worth investing my time and energy into. Healthy, long-term relationships of any kind require effort and consistency. By recognizing the areas that I struggle in maintaining those relationships I can be more aware in the future and avoid causing damage to them.

DECEMBER 28

Life may have mistakes, but it is important to not label those as failures in my eyes. Instead, I need to see each of those results as another chance to learn something about myself and life. Making the shift from a negative perspective—failure—to the positive one that is a learning opportunity will lead to more growth, more chances to learn, and have long-term benefits overall.

DECEMBER 29

I cannot let the pace of life dictate the speed at which I make decisions. When I give up that control, I lose the chance to prepare or to take time to consider the situation. The pressure from life's many stressful areas can make it incredibly hard to choose my speed over life's but in the end it will result in better choices and more productivity. The more it happens, the more confident I will become in choosing preparation over speed.

DECEMBER 30

I do not have an endless supply of emotional energy. By recognizing my limits, I will be more cognizant of where I invest that energy throughout the day. The more aware I am of this, the more I will be able to regulate the areas that deserve my energy and those that do not. Taking back control of my energy investment doesn't only increase how productive I can be, it also proves my worth to myself as I am my own priority.

DECEMBER 31

Being able to recognize myself for the things I accomplish is a very worthwhile practice to keep. I put effort and energy into the things I work towards, and because of this, I recognize that there is nothing wrong with celebrating myself. I began a journey one year ago and the fact that I am here now is something certainly worthy of recognizing. I will continue in that spirit and remember that I am valuable and the dedication I put into my goals is worthwhile as well!

Monthly Reflections

What did this last month mean to me?

What daily inspiration had the most meaning to me?

This month I learned...

Conclusion

As we move through life, it's easy to focus on how quickly time seems to pass. Days, weeks, months—before we know it, another year is gone. But what makes the difference isn't the time itself; it's how we choose to spend it. This year, you did something remarkable. You reclaimed moments for yourself, dedicated to reflection, growth, and the transformative power of positive affirmations.

Through this journey, you've achieved something much deeper than simply reading daily affirmations. You've taken meaningful steps toward understanding yourself better, identifying areas for growth, and building a stronger, more confident version of yourself.

Life may bring challenges and uncertainties that feel beyond our control, but what always remains within our power is the way we think and feel about ourselves. You've shown that it's possible to channel your energy toward constructive, empowering thoughts—beliefs that fuel your ability to rise above obstacles, embrace opportunities, and live with purpose.

What You've Achieved

This journal wasn't just a simple tool for self-care; it was your foundation for:

- **Cultivating Confidence**: You strengthened your belief in yourself, recognizing your ability to create positive change.
- **Fostering Self-Awareness**: You identified patterns, both helpful and limiting, and took steps to align your actions with your aspirations.
- **Taking Action**: You did more than reflect—you acted on your intentions, creating momentum for long-lasting growth.

And the best news? This journey doesn't end here.

A Continuous Pathway to Growth

This journal is designed to grow with you. It isn't something to be shelved or forgotten at the end of the year. You can revisit your entries to reflect on how far you've come—celebrate the goals you've achieved, acknowledge the lessons you've learned, and identify the areas where you want to keep growing.

As you move forward, consider starting a new journal for your next chapter. Each year offers new opportunities to deepen your self-awareness and continue building a life aligned with your values and dreams. Think of this as a cycle of reflection, action, and transformation—a process that evolves as you do.

Looking Ahead

What will you accomplish in the year ahead? What new habits will you develop, what goals will you set, and what positive changes will you create in your life? The next step is simple: continue doing what brought you here—reflect, act, and grow.

Take a moment to honor all that you've achieved. You didn't just make surface-level changes; you transformed deeply, creating a foundation for a future filled with possibility and purpose.

This is not an ending—it's a beginning.

Every new day is a blank page, waiting for you to write your story of growth, ambition, and self-discovery. Step into this next chapter with the same commitment and enthusiasm you've shown over the past year.

You've proven to yourself that you can create the life you desire. Now, the question is: what will the next chapter hold? The possibilities are endless. The journey continues, one step at a time, and it all starts with the same belief that guided you here—**empower your journey.**

THANK YOU!

Thank you for allowing this book to be a part of your journey toward self-discovery and personal growth. It is a privilege to provide you with daily affirmations that inspire and uplift, paired with space for your reflections, insights, and ideas. My hope is that this book becomes more than a tool—it becomes a companion, offering guidance and clarity as you unlock your full potential.

Every time you pause to reflect on an affirmation, you are taking a step closer to a more empowered and fulfilled version of yourself. I hope this book fills you with positivity and serves as a source of strength, helping you grow physically, mentally, and spiritually. Thank you for choosing this path of self-care and self-reflection, and for allowing me to contribute to your life in a meaningful way.

A Small Request

This book is the product of my passion, created with dedication and care. It was not backed by a large company or marketing team—I took on the journey of writing, producing, and bringing it to you independently. As such, I humbly ask for your support in sharing your thoughts about this book through a review.

Your review will not only help improve this book's visibility, allowing others to benefit from its affirmations, but it will also support independent authors like me in continuing to create resources that inspire and empower.

You can leave your review by scanning the QR code below.

Thank you again for your support, your time, and for being a part of this journey. Let's continue to grow, reflect, and thrive together, one day and one affirmation at a time.

Thank you very much in advance for your support!

Mauricio